20 KEYS TO WORKPLACE IMPROVEMENT

Revised Edition

20 Keys is the methodology for implementing PPORF (Practical Program of Revolutions in Factories).

PPORF is a simple improvement method with concrete and systematic steps for drastically reforming and strengthening every facet of the manufacturing organization.

20 KEYS TO WORKPLACE IMPROVEMENT

Revised Edition

Iwao Kobayashi

Publisher's Message by Norman Bodek

Productivity Press
Portland, Oregon

Originally published as *Zen-in sanka niyoru kōjō kakushin: Porufu jissenhō.*

Translated by Bruce Talbot. Appendix A translated by Miho Matsubara. Appendix C translated by Warren Smith.

Productivity, Inc.
P.O. Box 13390
Portland, OR 97213-0390
United States of America
Telephone: 503-235-0600
Telefax: 503-235-0909
E-mail: service@productivityinc.com

Cover design by William Stanton
Page design and composition by Matthew C. DeMaio
Graphics by Fineline Illustration and Matthew C. DeMaio
Printed and bound by Edwards Brothers in the United States of America

Library of Congress Cataloging-in-Publication Data
Kobayashi, Iwao
[Zen-in sanka niyoru kōjō kakushin: Porufu jissenhō. English]
20 keys to workplace improvement/Iwao Kobayashi—Revised edition
p. cm.
Translation of: Zen-in sanka niyoru kōjō kakushin: Porufu jissenhō (revision of Shokuba kaizen 20-kōmoku).
Includes index.
ISBN 1-56327-109-5 (hardcover)
1. Production management. 2. Industrial management. I. Title.
TS 155.K75513 1995
658.5–dc20 95-23802
CIP

02 01 00 99 10 9 8 7 6

Contents

Publisher's Message

One thing we have learned during more than a decade of observing companies trying to implement one manufacturing improvement approach or another is that these various approaches, applied individually, often don't lead to real, lasting improvement. The total level of operations and the ability to respond to customer needs often lag behind. Methods like quality control and team activities, which have great merit in themselves, nevertheless don't often produce the desired result. Why is this?

Companies that lead the world in their markets do so by improving more than one thing at a time, and by doing it over the long term. They recognize the importance of synergy between different improvement efforts and the need for commitment at all levels of the company to achieve total, systemwide upliftment.

The 20 Keys approach described in this book offers companies a way to look at the health of their manufacturing operations and to systematically upgrade it, level by level, through 20 different but interrelated aspects—all of which are addressed at once! To someone first hearing this, it might sound like an impossible amount of work. In reality, however, it is much more important to improve incrementally and simultaneously in all areas that support a world class operation than it is to improve a single key area, only to fall short when you realize that a critical supporting system is not in place.

The beauty of this book is its presentation of a system that defines the meaning of excellence in 20 key areas related to quality, delivery, and cost. It demonstrates how improvements in these areas actually work together to improve a company's overall competitiveness. Further, it shows you how to score your own company's progress through five levels in each key area and tells you how to plan a strategy for improving all the areas in an order that addresses your own particular needs. Most companies start out around 25 points (a little above level one in each key); according to 20 Keys creator Iwao Kobayashi, each subsequent 20-point improvement represents a 100 percent improvement in your productivity. In his revised book, you will find methods that apply not just to the shop floor, but also to administrative support areas, where waste often takes a big bite out of productivity.

The book begins with three foundational topics that pull together every level of the organization to prepare for future changes. Key 1, cleaning and organizing, is a fundamental beginning point that clears away clutter and arranges things so that you can spot problems and avoid wasteful searching and movement. Cleaning becomes a form of inspection that allows shopfloor workers to discover abnormalities and potential problems before they cause defects or breakdowns. These activities foster involvement, creating a unified purpose at a very basic level to make an environment that everyone in the company feels responsible for maintaining.

The second key, rationalizing the system/management of objectives, deals with aligning top management's improvement goals with the production floor's efforts to make it so. This is a critical point in any improvement program: determining the overall strategy for improvement, and then putting energy behind those strategic goals. Many companies' quality improvement movements have ended with disappointment when teams energetically pursued activities and targets that were not in sync with the management direction. Management, for its part, must plan for the long term and commit to a course long enough for results to manifest.

Key 3 is improvement team activities—the foundation upon which company-wide improvement is built. This key recognizes the communication, training, and support required to earn and maintain the trust, buy-in, and commitment of every employee of the company.

Building from these basic areas, the book moves on to help you gauge and improve your level in various focused improvement areas such as inventory and lead time reduction, quick changeover, value analysis, maintenance of equipment, supplier development and support, cross-training, use of computers, and conservation. The final key is a guided review of your own company's site technology, comparing it to that in other companies and to cutting-edge technology in your industry and beyond.

Author Iwao Kobayashi is one of Japan's best-known consultants, with more than three decades of manufacturing experience in industry and in private consulting. He has distilled all of this management learning into a big-picture approach he calls the Practical Program Of Revolutions in Factories (PPORF), known here as the 20 Keys System. In this book, Kobayashi makes his total-system expertise available to a wider audience in a highly usable form.

This revised edition is an updated and improved version of the 20 Keys book first published in 1990. Although the first edition has been widely used by managers throughout the Western world, Kobayashi originally intended it for shopfloor workers and teams. Feeling that managers needed more assistance with implementing the Keys, Kobayashi redrafted much of this book, inserting additional "half levels" in several of the keys to offer more detail on how to improve. Moreover, he has upped the ante throughout the book: Companies hoping to achieve level five must meet not only industry standards of excellence, but global standards. This is in keeping with the concept of benchmarking another company that is best in a critical process, regardless of the industry it is in; L.L. Bean's esteemed customer service is a frequently cited example.

New supplemental materials in the appendix include two case studies that bring the 20 Keys approach to life. Morioka Seiko Works, a member of the world class Seiko watch group, shares an interview with its president about how it came to implement a PPORF/20 Keys system, then talks about the kickoff and several important projects related to use of CAD/CAM and production-floor computers for parts changeovers in assembly. Windfall Products, a Pennsylvania-based leader in powder metal products, tells about how it adapted the 20 Keys program to meet its needs for a comprehensive improvement program with employee support.

Besides a completely new translation of Kobayashi's revised Japanese edition, this book also features a new page design that makes it easy to see the progression between the levels in each key. New cartoons lightheartedly illustrate each level.

20 Keys is a valuable tool for creating the total groundwork for a competitive breakthrough and ensuring that major targeted improvements don't fail for lack of necessary support in related areas. It is important to work on specific areas such as total productive maintenance, but long-term success requires a balanced approach over time. Think of it as a consciousness-raising investment to assure your company's competitive future.

This book is not an instant factory improvement kit containing every detail you need to improve in each area. You will need to be deeply involved in raising your company's performance in each key area. It may be that you need assistance or training to accomplish some aspects like quick changeover, effective computerization, or teamwork in maintenance and line improvements. Your own evaluation, based on the system presented here, will indicate the areas where you need help to achieve a higher score.

This book is valuable for your company, not just for the useful pointers at every level, but for the honest, wide-horizon look it requires you to give your own operations. I hope you will adopt its wisdom to become one of the top contenders in the twenty-first century.

We express our appreciation to Iwao Kobayashi for the privilege of publishing his books, and for his help in clarifying difficult points. Thanks as well to Nikkan

Kogyo Shimbunsha, the publisher of the Japanese edition of this book and also of the magazine in which the Morioka Seiko story first appeared. Eric Wolfe and Craig Feldbauer of Windfall Products kindly supplied their story for this edition. Productivity, Inc. consultant Charles Skinner was also very helpful in sharing his knowledge about 20 Keys implementations.

Many others also participated in creating this volume. Bruce Talbot translated the book from Japanese, and Warren Smith translated the Morioka Seiko case study. Thanks to Bob Shoemaker, president of Productivity, Inc., and to Barry Venter and Peter Wickens O.B.E. of Organisation Development International, for their advice and assistance. Thanks to Productivity Press staff members Steven Ott, president; Diane Asay, editor in chief; Karen Jones, editorial development; Mary Junewick and Angela Shoemaker, editorial support; Miho Matsubara, author liaison and translation support; Susan Swanson, production management; and Bill Stanton, cover design. Thanks also to Gordon Ekdahl of Fineline Illustration, cartoon graphics; Matthew DeMaio, page design, graphics, and composition; and Catchword, Inc., index.

Norman Bodek
Chairman

Preface to the Revised Edition

A dozen years have passed since the creation of the approach known as PPORF ("Practical Program Of Revolutions in Factories"), the 20 Keys approach described in this book. During this time, PPORF has been implemented all over Japan. Several hundred Japanese companies have received consulting in this approach and several thousand have attended PPORF seminars. Publications on PPORF and the 20 Keys have also spanned the globe in editions translated into English, French, Spanish, Italian, Korean, Chinese, Thai, and Tagalog. The system was introduced early in Southeast Asia and South Africa, where companies have already begun reporting success stories. Now this trend has begun to spread through Europe and North America.

Without exception, companies that have adopted PPORF's 20 Keys approach have achieved higher productivity as a result, as well as manufacturing quality that is flexibly responsive to change.

The previous edition of this book has become a best seller, with nearly 30,000 copies sold in Japan and 12,000 copies sold of the English-language edition. However, the earlier version was written primarily for equipment operators and other shopfloor employees. The present book is instead aimed at manufacturing managers and supervisors, offering specific lessons in how to effectively implement the 20 Keys system for the company as a whole. Like the original 20 Keys book, this volume is intended to be useful to a wide array of readers.

I offer my profound thanks to the people at the PPORF Development Institute of Eastern Japan, including Director Tanaka and Ms. Kazuko Miura, for their kind assistance in the production of this book.

Iwao Kobayashi

Introduction

PPORF: A Practical Program for Corporate Revolution

In the past several years, reengineering has become a new buzzword that generally refers to advances in management achieved by various large U.S. companies. However, reengineering is not a particular method but rather the trial-and-error application of various methodologies at numerous companies and consulting firms. This trial-and-error approach means that every sparkling tale of success reflects the many failures that have been stepping stones on the way.

In today's fast-changing industrial world, "factory revolution" aiming toward higher productivity and a stronger company has become a necessity for the stable, long-term development of manufacturing companies. To survive, companies must continually set and strive toward a variety of new goals.

Most of the "revolutionary" techniques proposed as part of reengineering are too difficult to implement or are likely to yield an inadequate, scattered effect of various incremental improvements. Although some improvement may be achieved, further efforts are stymied by insurmountable hurdles and/or a lack of direction for the future.

Factory revolution is a vague concept describing an activity that never seems to end. It is not an approach that can be followed vaguely, though. Furthermore, even though improvement can be endless, companies need targets for evaluation of past work and preparation for future work. We must set appropriate goals that suit our circumstances and we must also find the means for achieving those goals.

Today our economic environment is undergoing rapid change. Managers need to determine to what degree their companies can rapidly respond to change, and to regard such responsiveness as a standard for evaluating corporate strength. To have such a standard, they must have specific means of evaluation and specific items that can be improved. Managers cannot make their companies stronger unless they know how to improve items that assessment shows require improvement.

Evaluating the degree to which a manufacturing company can rapidly respond to change requires more than simply looking at a company's plant investment commitments. It also requires judging how strong and stable a company can remain while weathering change. Further, it requires recognition of key priorities at every level of the company, in the factories and among management.

The approach I have developed during more than four decades of guiding numerous companies in their efforts to change and improve is called PPORF (Practical Program Of Revolutions in Factories). The basic principles of PPORF implementation appear in the 20 Keys Relations Diagram below. The primary

20 Keys Relations Diagram

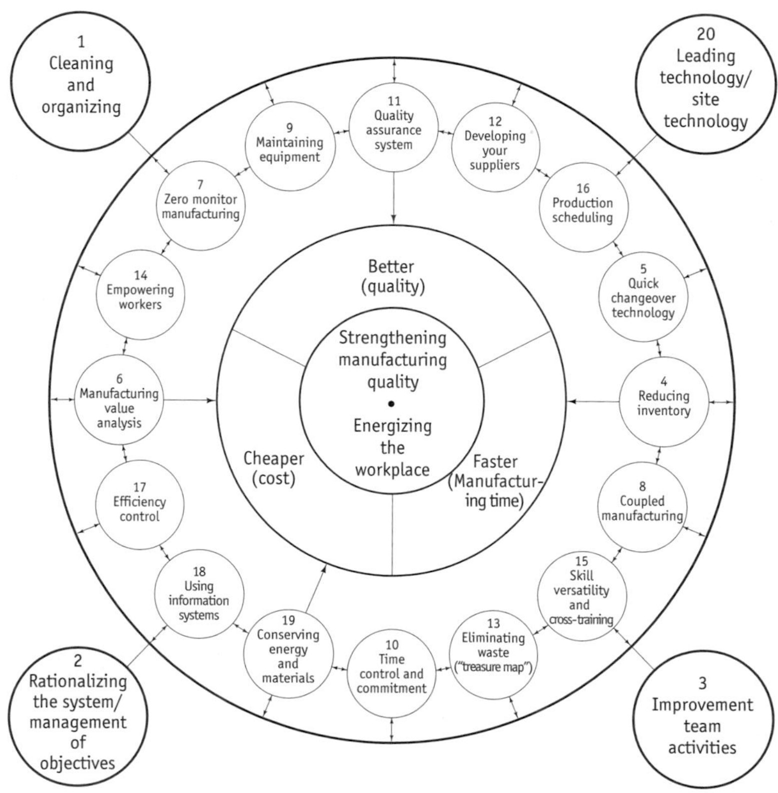

feature of PPORF is a scoring system for evaluating manufacturing strength known as the "20 Keys Five-Point Evaluation System."

Promoting Factory Revolution as a Total Package to Create Synergy

The 20 Keys system not only brings the world's manufacturing improvement methods together into one package but also integrates these separate methods into a closely interrelated whole. The result is a synergistic effect.

As suggested in the drawing below, applying conventional improvement methods one at a time may bring some initial gains, but over time obstacles crop up that make these methods harder to implement and their targets remain out of reach. By contrast, the PPORF approach integrates 20 key methods for "revolutionizing factories" into a balanced whole that can be implemented rationally and effectively. A structure supported by 20 pillars can still collapse if some of the pillars on one side are weak, but will remain strong if support is evenly balanced among

all 20 pillars. The "PPORF power" of 20 well-balanced keys pushes improvement to ever higher levels, achieving ever higher goals.

During the many public seminars I have given over the years, I have asked participants to score their companies in the 20 key areas. Average scores have ranged from 1.5 to 2.0 on a scale of 5. Analysis indicated that the companies I was teaching to use a 20 Keys approach (addressing their various improvement goals in an integrated way) were achieving increasingly higher scores, while little or no improvement was seen in companies that were not integrating the 20 keys into a synergistic whole.

The best way to implement the 20 keys differs from company to company. That is why consultants and implementers must provide guidance tailored to each organization.

People sometimes ask, "Isn't it difficult to implement so many keys at once?" My answer is that, because the 20 Keys are closely interrelated, making progress in one key automatically ties in with progress in the other 19. Synergistically, improvements in one key can be expected to produce positive effects in many other keys as well. After some progress in implementing the 20 Keys approach, individual improvements appear to create broad-ranging ripple effects. This is why progress is not difficult, even when addressing 20 subjects at once.

PPORF Aims to Boost Sales by Improving Customer Satisfaction

What kind of transformations can a company expect from adopting the 20 Keys? To create strong manufacturing quality and adaptability to change, the 20 Keys approach begins by ranking the workplace on a five-level scale, with level one designating the worst workplaces and level five the best, world class workplaces. This evaluation forms the standard by which subsequent improvement is measured.

However, the comparison here is not one company versus others in the same industry but rather one company versus others in all industries throughout the world. For example, a manufacturing company might be satisfied with keeping a two- to three-day supply of inventory, since that is what competing manufacturers generally do, but what if the company is compared to a produce company that keeps less than one day's inventory on hand? The point is that what passes as acceptable for your company's industry may be less than what your company can actually achieve to become truly strong and competitive.

When we consider other companies the world over, the highest-ranking companies in terms of quality, cost, and delivery (QCD) have reached very high levels indeed. But even some of these companies are obstructed by lack of a clear vision of what it takes to satisfy customers, like a cloud blocking the view from a mountain peak. Looking at competition on a global scale, the 20 Keys system combines a QCD approach (making products better, cheaper, and faster) with a customer-focused approach (making customers the next process) to create hit products. The 20 Keys system takes a hard look at customer satisfaction to create world class manufacturing quality.

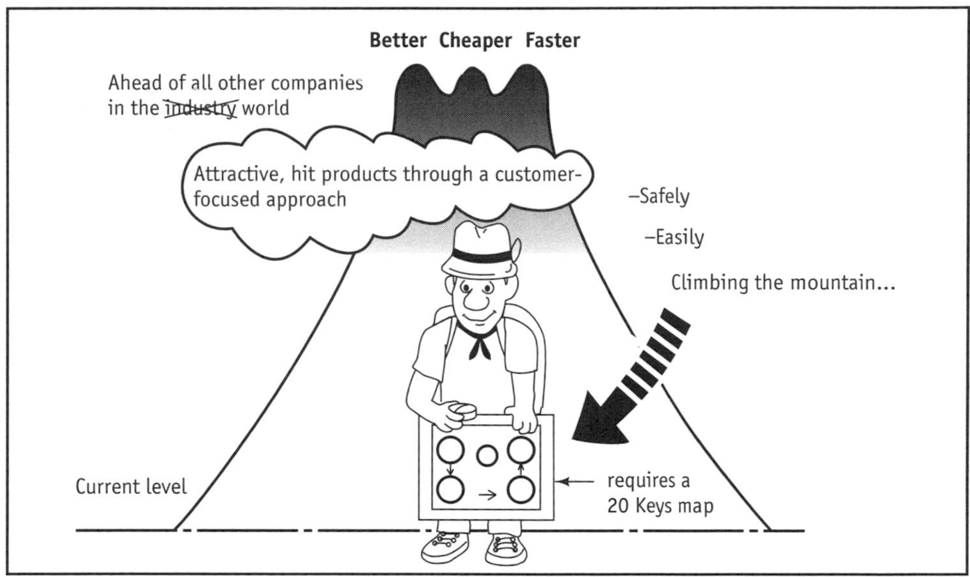

In today's industrial environment, when a company introduces a popular new product, now matter how novel, within six months or a year similar competing products will be on the market. By using the 20 Keys approach to improving manufacturing processes and shortening development periods, a company can move ahead of the competition worldwide in a way that makes it very difficult for other companies to catch up.

Synergy of 20 Keys Implementation

Let's think for a minute about what kind of program you would need to make better products more cheaply and quickly and with ensured safety and stability.

As in the drawing above, suppose you want to climb a mountain that has three peaks called Better, Cheaper, and Faster. Naturally, you want to climb it safely, too. You begin by evaluating your current level (let's assume you are evaluated at level two). Next, you need to think about how to climb. The quickest way might be the rockclimbing method, using ropes and technical gear. But that method takes a lot of effort and does not offer much support to those who follow you. If you are leading a group of climbers, it is better to create footholds as you go along so that your followers can climb more easily. It takes some effort to make all those footholds, but once they are done the mountain has a relatively easy path to follow.

The 20 Keys program is a way to make footholds all the way to the top of the manufacturing mountain, integrating the keys in a way that facilitates your company's ascent to the three pinnacles of manufacturing quality: Better, Cheaper, and Faster.

Looking over the 20 Keys Relations Diagram on page 2 will help you understand the interrelationships among the keys. The 4 keys outside the large circle support and stimulate the inner 16 keys, which in turn mutually support and stimulate each other. Eventually, the inner 16 keys also support and stimulate the outer 4 keys, so that all 20 keys are working synergistically to strengthen manufacturing quality.

The 20 Keys cover the factors every manufacturing company must consider. Depending on the particular conditions and characteristics, companies may give priority to certain keys over others, and the order in which the keys are implemented may differ. Although the combinations of priorities and implementation sequences are almost limitless, the proper combination becomes apparent as you better understand the keys.

After initial education about the program, the first step is to have frontline workers evaluate themselves in each of the 20 Keys, within groups or sections if necessary. As they attempt to grade their own work groups, they discover their relative strengths and weaknesses, and this tends to pique their interest in making improvements.

After grading themselves in each of the keys, they begin to see the mutual relationships among the keys, and this helps them determine which keys to address first. Generally, companies have taken on about seven of the keys each year, so that in three years they will have taken on the productivity-boosting challenge of implementing all 20 keys.

Strategic Goals and Tactical Goals

Some managers worry that introducing a new program such as 20 Keys would cause confusion, since their factories are already implementing some other goal-oriented program.

Others worry that meeting the challenge of any one of the 20 Keys is hard enough, and taking on all 20 would be simply impossible. The problem with these arguments is that they come from an erroneous perspective.

The 20 Keys program in fact lays a foundation that makes existing management goals easier to achieve and more likely to be maintained over time. Moreover, it can be implemented as a mid-range business plan lasting about three years and aimed toward specific strategic goals. To fully achieve the company's business goals for each term—what we might call its tactical goals—the company must create the organizational strength to succeed at these challenges, and that is where the 20 Keys program comes in.

Most companies report that the pace of improvement-making efforts tends to slow down when the deadline for previous goals has passed and the new goals have just been set. The 20 Keys program avoids this problem by creating one big movement of improvement-making that lasts about three years (for all 20 keys) while still allowing measurement of the improvements made during each term. In other words, instead of treating term-specific goals as tactical goals (i.e., separate objectives), the 20 Keys program treats them as strategic goals (goals that are integrated into an overall strategy).

Improvement in the 20 Keys Means Improvement in Productivity

Japanese companies usually measure productivity in terms of labor, such as the number of product units produced per employee labor-hour or the number of employees needed to operate a particular machine.

If we apply this definition to, for example, Key 6 (Value Analysis of Manufacturing Operations), improving a department's score from level two to level four would require cutting the number of labor-hours in half, thereby doubling productivity. However, to make such a productivity improvement, the company must also develop what it needs to smoothly boost productivity in today's competitive business climate, which would include quality and delivery issues. In other words, to create the footholds it needs to climb from level two to level four, the company must also deal with issues related to the other 19 keys.

Case studies of companies that have improved themselves via the 20 Keys show that by generally applying the 20 Keys program—which includes addressing their areas of greatest need—these companies have managed to greatly improve their productivity. For example, a factory that scored 50 points at the start improved to 70 points and another factory went from 60 to 80 points. Each company combines the elements of the 20 Keys program according to its own needs.

A Word about Safety

Although injuries often occur in unpredictable situations, daily attention to improvement through the 20 Keys can work wonders in making everyone more safety-conscious and creating accident-free workplaces. Whenever you analyze the cause of an accident, you will find something that ties in with one of the 20 Keys, such as "happened due to dirt and disorganization," "occurred when defective goods were being produced," or "occurred under strenuous work conditions." All 20 Keys relate in some way to the issue of safety. Companies that want to systematically minimize safety hazards should regard the 20 Keys approach as an absolute necessity.

Key 1

Cleaning and Organizing

One might expect to start with Key 2's "Rationalizing the System/Management of Objectives." However, 4S activities (referring to the initials of the Japanese words for various aspects of standardized industrial housekeeping) are a critical foundation for success in the other 19 keys. 4S is therefore rightfully Key 1.

The first two 4S elements, cleaning and organizing, are an issue in every workplace. Even though cleaning and organizing are basic to good working conditions, they are seldom implemented thoroughly, so problems remain. Even when the process of maintaining a clean and organized workplace has been simplified, there's an oversight here, a shortcut there, and soon workplace conditions are as bad as ever.

The 20 Keys approach solves this problem by making the 4Ss something workers want to do to make their work easier rather than something they perceive as being forced upon them. Workplace employees should plan how the 4Ss will be implemented by discussing what currently makes their work harder and what can be done to make it easier. This helps build a common awareness of 4S issues.

When implementing the 4Ss, it is important to make solid improvements one level at a time, such as from level one to level two or level two to level three. The 20 Keys approach starts and ends with the 4Ss. Once the 4Ss have been implemented, it is easier to implement the other 19 keys. Conversely, as progress is made in the other keys, it becomes easier to maintain the 4Ss. Remember—it is vital not only to implement the 4Ss but also to maintain them to prevent backsliding.

Level One

Cigarette butts, scrap paper, and tools and parts are left scattered.

Even today, there are many companies with messy workplaces. If you look at workplaces that managers claim are litter-free, other forms of litter can still be found—they need to rethink what "litter" really means. What about tools, jigs, manuals, and even machines and equipment that remain on site even though they haven't been used in months or years? Such items should be stored or disposed of.

When I inspect workplaces for unnecessary clutter, I often find signs that are outdated or worn and dirty. When such signs stay up, people are unlikely to notice the newer signs.

When surveying offices, I have come across plenty of desks covered with an untidy array of books, pens, and papers. When I see a desk like that, I know that its owner wastes time looking for things. Some desks hold overflowing ashtrays, with some long-forgotten papers underneath. Boxes are piled with books stacked on their sides so their titles cannot be read. Workplaces like this are definitely ranked "level one."

Level Two

Dispose of unneeded items.

Keep the floors clean.

At level two, the workplace might appear neat and clean at first glance, but if you look around you'll find an amazing amount of unneeded items piled on desks, shelves, and/or machines. Such workplaces need to be gone over: ask whether each item is scheduled for use today or, at most, within the next week. If it will not be used by then, move it out or get rid of it. It is better to store such things elsewhere, even though they may have to be brought back sometime. Anything that has gone unused for even one month should be treated as unneeded. In offices, that includes extra pencils and erasers that accumulate in desk drawers. If you gather up all these extra items (extra usually means "more than one"), you will be amazed at the huge stockpile of usable supplies that results.

Also at level two, work-in-process (WIP) and tools are piled neatly, but the piles are right on the floor. This means that before these items can be used, someone has to bend over and pick them up. They are also difficult to move elsewhere and therefore tend to get in the way. Getting rid of all floor piles is one way to make work easier.

Important Points

- Don't leave items on the floor.
- Get rid of things that will not be used soon.

Problems at Level Two

Look at how things are placed.

The workplace is now at level two, but if you look at the corners, especially where the floor meets walls or pillars, you will find unneeded items, dirt, or dust. Such items are also likely to accumulate along or behind large equipment units. Notice also that pathways are not outlined and so piles of stuff stick out into walking or transport paths.

Perhaps some white tape or paint was once used to mark pathways but over time the markings have worn away in places. Or maybe your workplace is supposed to be all "work area" with no marked pathways. All workplaces should have well-marked pathways. Plan a new layout and make some pathways as soon as possible.

You can probably find some work-in-process or empty boxes that are poorly organized. If products, WIP, tools, or other items are in cartons sitting directly on the floor, move the cartons to a position that makes them more easily accessible.

In offices, the power cords and cables from computers, fax machines, copiers, and other equipment can be found all over the backs or sides of desks like well-tossed spaghetti. Instead, they should all be bundled and routed inconspicuously.

Level Three

Clean up equipment.

Mark pathways and clear out the corners.

Have the employees paint all parts of the walls and pillars that can be reached by hand (up to about six and a half feet). Painting requires cleaning off dirt and dust. Use a bright color so that everyone can stand and see fresh new paint all around them at eye level. If it takes two or three coats of paint to get the workplace looking bright and clean, so be it. The equipment should be sparkling clean and spotless: clean equipment is easier to maintain and less likely to break down.

Make special-purpose carts or pallets to hold various kinds of work-in-process. These carts or pallets should not be stored randomly, but should have clearly assigned, well-planned places. Design them so that it is easy to take items off and put them back in the right place. If items need to go in at certain angles, indicate those as well.

Important Points

- Clearly determine and mark off areas that each work group is responsible for (including pathways).
- Have regular "check-up inspections" where work groups engage in friendly competition to be the best.

Problems at Level Three

Look at what is on tables and shelves.

Now pathways are clear and distinctly marked and the floors and walls are also clean. However, tabletops, cabinets, and shelves are still cluttered with a hodge-podge of parts, tools, rags, gauges, books, and other items. There are no clearly marked places for work-in-process, and sometimes it is hard to find needed tools.

Open the doors of storage cabinets and what do you find? Chances are that a lot of unused stuff has been crammed in there. The rationale in locking things away is that they will be safe there. But it is more important to create a workplace where tools can be easily found and retrieved.

Level Four

Clearly organize and mark all sections using right angles and parallel lines.

Organize storage areas for each workstation.

Use labeling, numbering, or color-coding to indicate exactly which tools (or jigs, parts, gauges, cleaning supplies, etc.) go where. This makes these items easy to find and put back correctly. Organize items neatly, using right angles and parallel lines wherever possible. Keep high-use tools, gauges, and the like within easy reach. Organize items on shelves by function and mark them so anyone can tell what any machine, part, tool, or manual is used for. In offices, this applies to filing systems: Files should be easy for anyone to locate.

Remove doors from cabinets so contents are always visible. The contents should be well organized and labeled. Set up special carts to hold work-in-process and tools on visible shelves so workers can find and retrieve items within three seconds.

In a level-four workplace each person can work easily and efficiently, with a minimum of motion needed to pick up parts, tools, and other items.

Important Points

- Organize tools and parts separately for each workstation.
- Use a labeling, numbering, or color-coding system for shelf storage.

Problems at Level Four

Make sure the workplace stays clean and well organized.

Although workstations are now organized so that people can reach everything they need with simple motions, they find it hard to keep it orderly and tend to let things slide until right before inspection. This kind of workplace soon receives lower scores in the other 19 keys.

Also, shelf storage has been organized so everyone knows what goes where, but it is hard to tell when supplies are low and should be reordered. This increases the risk of unexpected shortages.

Third, brooms and other cleaning equipment are on hand for workers to clean up chips and other debris between jobs. However, this debris piles up during each job and things get pretty messy before people can clean up.

In offices, files, papers, and other "work-in-process" piles up each day, giving the place a disorganized look.

Corrective Action to Get to Level Five

Earn a perfect score even during surprise inspections.

Mark stock levels clearly.

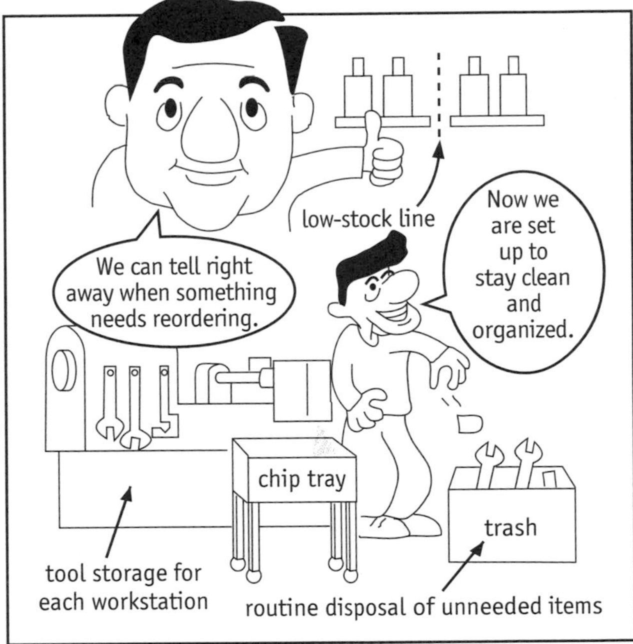

Set up a system like supermarkets use for clearly indicating low stock levels. Store parts and other supplies in a way that facilitates automatic reordering when quantities reach a certain level.

Identify exactly what causes things to get dirty and address those causes. For example, if chips and shavings pile up next to a lathe, install a tray or basket to catch the debris before it hits the floor. Organize parts using carts or fixtures that make it easy to keep them in proper order when not in use.

When various workgroups compete to achieve and maintain level-four status, being clean and well organized becomes habitual so that eventually the workplace will receive perfect scores even during surprise inspections.

Important Points

- Hold routine inspections every month and develop the habit of being clean and well organized.
- Devise ways to automatically dispose of chips, worn tools, and other trash.

Level Five

Eliminate causes of dirt and disorder.

At level five, the causes of dirt and disorder have been eliminated as much as possible. As a result:

- The workplace stays clean without much sweeping or wiping.
- Storage sites and quantities are clearly marked.

At this level, not only is the workplace fully clean and organized but everyone has learned the habit of keeping it that way by periodically clearing out unneeded items.

The 4Ss are now being maintained in every corner of the workplace. This has made everyone's work easier and safer. Consequently productivity is up, defects and customer claims are down, delivery periods are shorter, and there is more open floor space.

The flow of operations is easy to see now. Each process is now clean and well organized.

Now you can see how the other 19 keys rest on the foundation of the 4Ss. Maintaining the 4Ss means maintaining the conditions for a new production system in which products are made better and more cheaply, quickly, and safely.

Key 2

Rationalizing the System/ Management of Objectives

The convergence of top-down and bottom-up management for a more rational organization.

International competition and economic volatility have thrust major changes on many manufacturers, in many cases forcing them to implement radically different policies to adapt quickly. To implement such abrupt policy changes, a company usually must follow a top-down approach to decision making.

However, following the top-down approach alone can make it difficult to achieve goals. When top management issues policies and expects others to follow through, they will fail unless the followers also feel the goal is their own. Goals are more attainable when everyone owns them and helps each other reach them. Only through a cooperative convergence of top-down and bottom-up decision making can an organization become truly adaptive to change

The first requirement in implementing the 20 Keys is that everyone agrees to work together toward success. Key 2 helps top managers and frontline managers work together to set goals, own those goals, and pursue them diligently.

It is fitting that Key 2 is situated like an anchor at the bottom left of the 20 Keys Relations Diagram. A vital part of any 20 Keys improvement plan is an annual meeting of executives and frontline managers to set goals and agree on how to achieve them.

Level One
Chain-Gang Style

No clear management system.

If you visit a chain gang working at a prison camp, you'll probably hear the gang boss barking orders, such as "now start digging" or "get that wheelbarrow over here." Naturally, the laborers hate this work and are apprehensive about what's next. In a company, managers still have to set the direction for the work, but there are ways to avoid the "chain gang" environment. The level-one workplace has the following characteristics:

- Each set of operations begins with instructions given by a superior.
- Managers don't care how well each worker performs the assigned tasks.
- Workers sometimes receive contradictory instructions from their boss's boss.
- Workers look for reasons to avoid challenging assignments rather than striving to achieve them.
- Frontline managers and workers have little idea of what is going on in other parts of the company. As a result, there is duplication of labor.

Level-one workplaces such as this can be found in parts of many companies of various sizes. Having workers simply respond to verbal orders may look like a fast way to get work done. However, even more is to be gained by improving workplace management to higher levels.

Level Two

Make an organization chart and specify details.

Ideas and improvements are easier to generate when a company has a clear organizational structure. By contrast, you can't hope for much improvement when instructions are given ad hoc, differing for each workplace or employee. If a workplace lacks a clear organizational structure, the first task is to write down the current main responsibilities of each employee.

- Make a function-based organization chart reflecting current responsibilities.
- Revise the chart to eliminate duplication of responsibilities and to fill gaps.

The following conditions must be established to attain level two:

1. Each person's range of responsibilities is clearly defined.
2. The individual responsibilities are clearly described.
3. The chain of authority is clearly defined.
4. Employees have a positive attitude about following instructions.
5. The rules of the organization are clearly expressed.

Problems at Level Two

"Safety First" Style

Top management's goals are clearly defined, but middle and lower managers are not sure what they really mean.

At level two, the company has a well-defined organization chart, with clearly stipulated rules and regulations. However, instructions from top management are not always understood well. For example, suppose top management issues a policy of "Safety First." Middle managers turn around and tell their subordinates, "Safety comes first!" without further explanation. Likewise, it is futile for top managers to issue instructions to "make good products cheaper and faster" if middle managers are simply going to parrot the words without really understanding them. The shopfloor employees end up wondering exactly what the instructions mean and how in the world they can follow them. This phenomenon is surprisingly common.

The chain of authority to be clarified within the organizational structure is not like a military chain of command. The organization should be flexible. People from every level should feel free to contribute ideas. This is particularly true of safety concerns—whoever notices a hazard should speak up directly and immediately. The 20 Keys approach empowers employees at all levels to share the same goals and to exercise their ingenuity in devising methods to achieve those goals.

Level Three
Clockwork Style

Instructions from top management are broken down into more detail at each level of the organization.

At level three, top management directives are broken down into more specific objectives at each lower level of management, like the way gears interconnect in a clockwork mechanism. Each department is clearly instructed in its responsibilities, and objectives at each level are detailed. For example, if top management says "Safety First," department managers translate this into safety-related areas such as fire prevention and they instruct the next level to make sure there are enough fire extinguishers. Section managers, in turn, consider what kind of fire extinguishers are needed and instruct their subordinates to buy them. Shopfloor managers then make sure everyone knows how to use the equipment.

As applied to corporate targets set by top management:

1. Top management objectives are clearly described at each level of the organization.
2. The objectives are broken into more specific objectives at each successive level.
3. Graphs are created and posted to show the specific objectives of each department, section, and workgroup.
4. Managers at each level monitor the graphed progress toward the objectives, giving feedback to the employees.

Problems at Level Three

Goals are set but are not well coordinated and cooperation among employees is lacking.

At level three, the company has established the kind of "management of objectives" most companies pursue. This is a basic stage for company organizations, and it was very popular during the high-growth era. Nevertheless, it is still a top-down, clockwork-style approach and poses a dilemma for companies now in a slow-growth phase, when ambitious executive objectives sometimes are too difficult to achieve.

In this situation, employees feel like cogs in the wheel—objectives are forced on them, like it or not. Naturally, they look for reasons why the objectives can't be reached. Middle managers pass the buck by assigning the hardest tasks to others.

Authority may flow downward through the organization, but work flows sideways. For example, a manager at an upstream process in a production line may decide that it will improve efficiency to switch the process from mixed, small-lot production to large-lot production. Consequently, the next downstream process keeps getting the same parts in large quantities and starts running out of other parts. This lack of lateral coordination makes it hard to improve the production line as a whole or to reach current objectives.

Level Four

Baseball Style

Management levels work cooperatively in setting objectives and coordinate their efforts to achieve common goals.

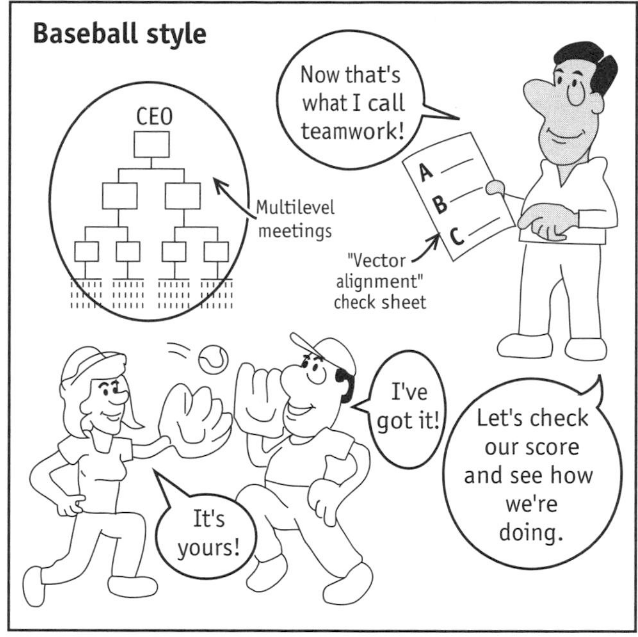

At level four, managers at different levels work together to set appropriate goals. Consequently, everyone owns the goals and coordinates their efforts to achieve them. Level four requires the following kinds of "baseball-style" teamwork:

1. Each factory and each section conducts a 20 Keys evaluation.
2. All managers study the company's basic policies and get a clear idea of the 20 Keys and how they interrelate.
3. Multilevel meetings are held to clarify basic policies and review the past year's progress.
4. Objectives based on the basic policies are set as numerical targets, and actual results are later displayed along with planned results.
5. Departments and sections assist each other when necessary.
6. Everyone gains experience in how the 20 keys interrelate and enjoys their synergistic effects.
7. A midterm multilevel meeting is scheduled to launch plans for the second half of the year.
8. The company strives to achieve at least 80 percent of the targets by the midterm meeting.
9. Offices and other staff departments pursue their own 20 Keys program modeled on similar basic policies.
10. The past year's results are presented annually at multilevel meetings, and at least 80 percent of the goals have been achieved.

Problems at Level Four

Watch for groups that are having trouble achieving their goals.

The multilevel meetings are held in part to "align vectors," which means to make sure that the company's goals and the employees' goals are the same so that everyone is working in the same direction.

Despite semiannual meetings to harmonize company goals, changes such as market trends can alter the conditions under which the goals are pursued.

You need to observe whether the groups are achieving 100 percent of the objectives. If certain groups are having trouble—including nonmanufacturing departments and supplier companies—other groups should lend a hand. Make sure everyone understands how the 20 Keys interrelate and work synergistically.

Level Five

All-Weather Style

Be prepared to deal with changing conditions in the pursuit of your goals.

Work to create common goals, improve individual skills, and boost teamwork toward company-wide objectives.

At level five, executives and frontline managers feel they have the same objectives, and these objectives are spelled out as numerical targets. The organization encourages top-down and bottom-up teamwork. Each person is encouraged to improve his or her abilities, and the entire company has a cooperative, "all for one and one for all" spirit.

People must work to achieve goals under changing conditions. When everyone in the company works as a team, they are much more able to adapt to whatever changes occur in their environment.

Level Five

All-Weather Style (continued)

Midterm and long-term objectives of the 20 Keys are understood by people in sales, R&D, and affiliates and suppliers, as well as manufacturing managers.

The 20 Keys system is not just for top managers to learn about: everyone should have an idea of the mid- and long-term objectives of the company. The 20 Keys objectives are not just for manufacturing managers but also for people in sales, R&D, and other departments, as well as managers in affiliated and supplier companies.

1. At least 80 percent of the goals are achieved by the midterm multilevel meeting.
2. 100 percent are achieved by the year-end multilevel meeting.
3. 20 Keys activities extend beyond the manufacturing department to include other departments as well as affiliates and supplier companies.
4. 100 percent goal achievement is expected not only from manufacturing but also from sales and R&D.
5. Everyone in the company knows the midterm and long-term 20 Keys objectives and plans.
6. Company objectives and employees' objectives are identical.
7. The company can adapt promptly to environmental changes.

Key 3

Improvement Team Activities

Improvement team activities support company goals.

Key 3 is at the bottom right of the 20 Keys Relations Diagram on page 2. Like Key 2, it has an anchoring position that reflects the importance of team activities in improving manufacturing quality. The invigoration of workplace morale through team activities creates a competitive strength quite different from the strength gained through effective management of objectives. Improvement teams composed of frontline workers use their hands-on expertise to set appropriate targets that deal with the work environment, human relations issues, and other issues.

Team-based improvement activities have trouble when company and team objectives are different. Teams need to work on issues that matter to management as well as to their own jobs. When the 20 Keys program is fully implemented, frontline workers are able to clearly express their objectives as scores, and they find it much easier to determine which improvement topics deserve immediate attention. The 20 Keys system harmonizes upper and lower management goals, which strengthens team activities and encourages improvement suggestions from everyone.

Level One

Employees have no desire to get involved in team activities.

When frontline employees hear words like, "You know what you're supposed to do, so get to work!" it's a put-down—it makes them feel like slaves. This creates a backlash in which people try to do as little work as possible. On the other hand, giving free rein to workers to determine their own work methods runs the risk of confusing the ease of efficiency with the ease of idleness. Neither condition fosters enthusiastic employee participation in team-based improvement activities. Level-one companies lack supportive conditions for improvement activities.

Level Two

An employee suggestion system is established.

The company gets involved in starting team activities.

Improvement suggestions climb to at least six per employee each year.

An improvement suggestion system is a good way to get improvement teams started. Devise forms employees can use to submit improvement ideas, and give simple rewards for good proposals. Start by creating forms that are easy to understand and fill out, and hold meetings to explain the suggestion system and encourage participation. Some employees may be uncomfortable trying to express their ideas, so supervisors should offer assistance as needed.

Managers evaluating suggestions should recognize both the potential improvement effects of each suggestion and the work that went into preparing it. That way, the suggestion system will be people-oriented as well as performance-oriented—a twofold orientation that has synergistic effects. However, a suggestion system alone is not enough to motivate the active participation of some people, especially those who feel incapable of useful suggestions. One way to overcome this is to form workplace teams to compete in a "suggestion tournament" for the most improvement ideas.

Important Points

- Make the suggestion system both performance-oriented and people-oriented.

Problems at Level Two

Employees lack enthusiasm for personal improvement.

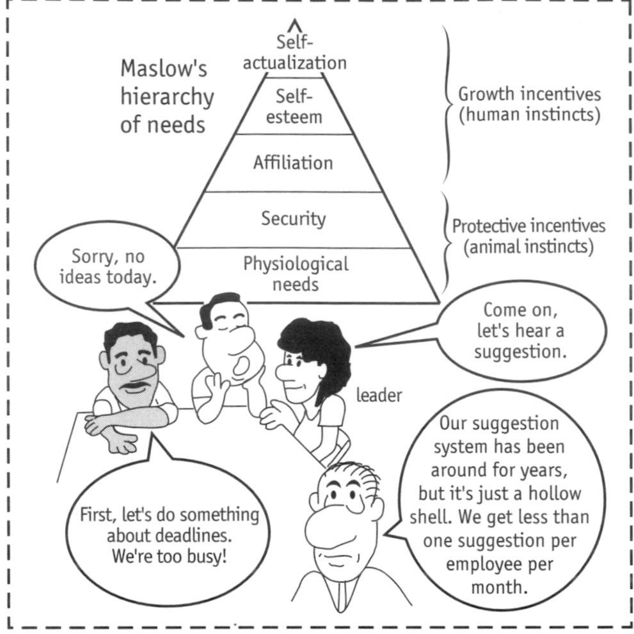

In level-two companies, employees clearly lack enthusiasm for personal improvement (called self-actualization in Maslow's hierarchy of needs). Such enthusiasm is not likely to exist unless it is based on empowerment of employees to pursue the challenges that really interest them. Improvement teams should not be assigned targets to work toward—they should devise their own. If improvement teams are merely subunits of the existing organizational structure, such as workplace groups led by their immediate supervisors, team members will feel like pawns asked to do extra work to meet someone else's goals.

It is pointless for team leaders to pressure members to come up with ideas. If they do, they are likely to get responses like the ones illustrated here. Instead, team members must first understand how team activities serve their own desires for personal improvement and self-actualization.

Level Three

Team activities are based on autonomous improvements.

Groups complete at least two improvement projects per year.

Each member submits at least one improvement suggestion per month.

At level three, frontline employees start improvement teams. They set their own goals, including process and human relations improvements, then apply their experience and energy toward reaching them. Some key points for promoting team activities:

1. Form teams of three to seven people from the same workplace.
2. The leader guides discussion and consensus. Choose the first leader, then rotate the role among the members. The team also determines roles for each member in implementing improvements.
3. Each team selects the most important improvement topics from member suggestions. The goal is to complete at least two improvement projects per year. At the end of the year, a presentation is held to announce results and honor successful teams.

These steps will help teams attain the goal of at least one improvement suggestion per month per member. An awards party or other fun event will also stir up enthusiasm.

Important Point

- Hold frequent, short meetings during work hours. Stand-up meetings keep things brief and focused.

Problems at Level Three

Dedicated support from managers is a must.

Level-three teams start out full of autonomous enthusiasm, but over time they find it hard to devise useful improvement topics or they have trouble selecting objectives that are both employee-oriented and company-oriented. Consequently, their achievements become less important and increasingly they are just going through the motions of making improvements. To head off such a trend, teams need dedicated support and encouragement from managers.

The 20 Keys system provides a wide range of ideas teams can consider before selecting improvement topics. When a company implements the 20 Keys, it sets an action plan and specific action items for each key. These action items point to good, challenging improvement topics. Moreover, team topics that relate to action items are guaranteed to mesh with management objectives, which makes managers more likely to support team projects. This is the synergy produced when team goals are both performance-oriented and people-oriented. The result is an atmosphere of employee empowerment.

Important Points

- Team meetings during work hours must be brief and efficient. Meetings held after work can be relaxed and casual.
- Managers should lend personal support to after-work meetings as well as daytime meetings.

Level Four

Improvement topics combine employee goals with company goals and include "vector alignment."

Improvement teams complete at least four improvement themes per year.

Team members submit at least two suggestions per month.

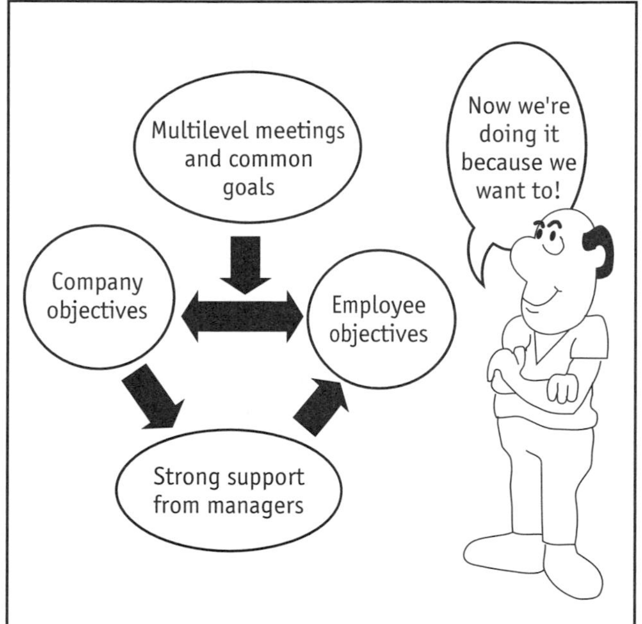

At level four, improvement topics align the vectors of management and employee improvement activities to combine employee goals with company goals. Thanks to system rationalization as part of Key 2, the mechanism of multilevel meetings has been established, whereby employees at various organizational levels can meet and establish common goals.

As the interrelations of the 20 Keys become clear, it is easier to understand improvement objectives. Better understanding promotes better communication, which in turn aids vector alignment so that the topics selected by improvement teams will be objectives that serve the entire company.

Eventually, team activities will go smoothly without much support from management and team members can be justly proud of their self-made successes. This serves the employees' desire for self-fulfillment and further invigorates team activities.

Problems at Level Four

There are still 17 keys to be implemented.

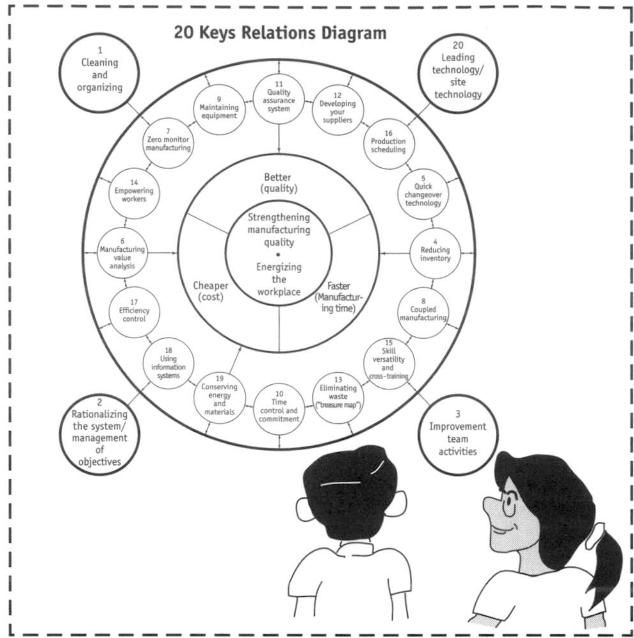

At this stage, the company still has 17 keys left to implement. However, improvement team activities are definitely the most effective means of specifically implementing these keys for the overall strengthening of manufacturing quality.

Once everyone is familiar with the 20 Keys and how they interrelate, they can use them as a guide as they devise worthwhile objectives that are suitable for team activities.

Nevertheless, even the most enthusiastic teams can lose their spark if they perceive managers to be indifferent about team activities. When a group encounters particularly difficult problems, managerial and technical assistance may be needed to prevent frustration from dampening enthusiasm. Managers can get involved in training sessions and multilevel meetings to keep in touch with team activities and help them proceed smoothly and effectively.

Important Point

- Make sure everyone understands the 20 Keys and their interrelations.

Level Five

After-work activities where people can relax and enjoy themselves promote mutual understanding and help align team goals with company goals.

The workplace has been invigorated and everyone is enthusiastic about improvement teams. Once a company has firmly adopted the 20 Keys approach, teams are likely to stay vigorous for decades. This is because an environment beneficial to everyone has been created: employees at all levels recognize their interdependence and are working together toward common goals.

In this environment, team activities are regularly successful, and as soon as one goal is reached, the team is already thinking excitedly about the next. Morale is continually boosted through after-work activities that enable employees to relax and get to know each other better.

This is the kind of workplace environment that characterizes a level-five company.

Level Five

(continued)

Improvement team activities are active and enthusiastic.

Teams average at least six completed themes per year.

Team members average at least five suggestions per month.

The Role of Team Activities in Companywide Improvement

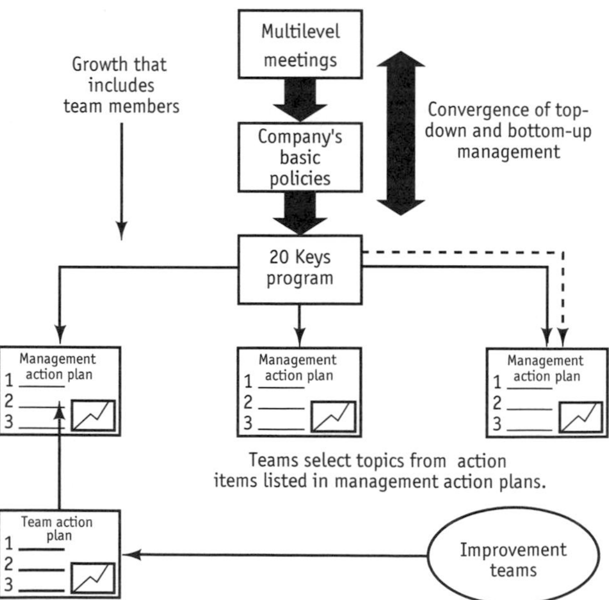

Key 4

Reducing Inventory (Shortening Lead Time)

Enlisting employee enthusiasm toward reducing work-in-process.

Shortening production lead time is the most important aspect of managing short-term orders that contain a wide variety of product specifications. Shortening the lead time at all stages from processing orders to product development, design, production, and shipment is certain to boost customer satisfaction.

Work-in-process (in-process inventory, or WIP) is a major cause of long lead times. WIP ranges from raw materials to finished products. It eats up assets and space as well as the labor involved in managing it and transporting it and the materials used in storing it—hence the saying that "inventory is the root of all evil." There are limits to reducing WIP—some material is always in processing—but if a factory can cut its WIP in half, it can also reduce its delivery period by half.

In cutting WIP and lead times, executives, managers, and operators all have opinions on how to do it. Without consensus on the approach, efforts will fail. It is crucial for those involved to develop a method they can all follow to ensure success.

In offices and staff departments, paperwork WIP can be reduced to remove administrative bottlenecks and make operations smoother and faster. Like production processes, clerical processes can be rearranged to greatly reduce cycle times.

Level One

Work-in-process is considered a "necessary evil."

People are not very concerned about reducing it.

In the level-one factory, people think that when deliveries fall behind, the line can be accelerated by feeding in more materials, thereby prompting the workers to work faster. As a result, work-in-process piles up everywhere, and employees end up spending extra time and labor taking care of it. Not knowing any better, managers think, "It can't be helped. We just need to work harder."

Under such conditions, discrepancies easily arise between the inventory records and WIP on hand. If actual WIP doesn't match the records, it is difficult to use a computer-based system such as MRP to issue production orders. Moreover, managing the WIP takes at least one or two days of production lead time.

Level-one factories are likely to have more "rush" lots due to the slow pace of normal lots, which causes more confusion as expedited lots are moved ahead. This further slows the pace of regular production and results in even bigger piles of backed-up WIP.

In level-one offices, desks are piled randomly with files and papers, and busy workers spend a lot of time looking for things. Such conditions slow down processing and make it easier to misplace or mistakenly discard documents.

Corrective Action to Get to Level Two

Everyone must understand that reducing WIP makes work easier and is the main factor in reducing waste.

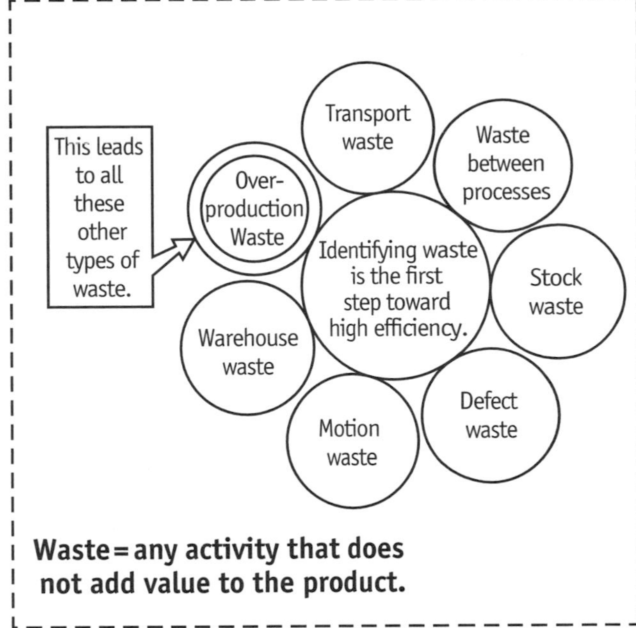

The fastest way to identify waste is to eliminate the overproduction that gives rise to the other types of waste. In processes with large amounts of WIP, the availability of extra materials hides problems with defects and abnormalities, since there is no wait for more workpieces. Reducing WIP removes that cushion, so defects and equipment problems must be addressed.

Work-in-process creates extra work (i.e., waste) in transporting, loading and unloading, and storing inventory, making factory work in general more difficult. If you can reduce WIP, there is less to handle, less to do to clean and organize the factory, and less chance of misplacing things. If everyone understands this, it will be easier to launch an effective inventory reduction campaign and create a better work environment.

Important Points

- Waste is any activity that does not add value to the product.
- Reducing overproduction waste (WIP) makes all other forms of waste easier to identify.

Level Two

Inventory reduction campaigns are launched in pilot areas.

Inventory has been reduced in at least one part of each factory.

In factories with no direct experience in reducing inventory, trying to suddenly do it everywhere will only cause massive confusion. To avoid such confusion, start with a pilot site, then move laterally to ensure solid progress.

Start by selecting one process or line as the pilot. Selecting just one site will make it easier to manage the various problems that will come up when the extra WIP is removed.

Once inventory has been reduced and the other problems solved on the pilot line, it becomes an effective demonstration site for the entire workplace. Better yet, if a pilot line can be established for each type of operation (in manufacturing, clerical, etc.), all employees can see how inventory reduction can make their work easier. Companies that have come this far are at level two.

Offices can reduce inventory by various methods, such as limiting desktop paperwork to the amount that fits into a single transparent tray with a line to show the maximum amount.

Important Point

- The fewer the trays, the better the flow of paperwork.

Corrective Action to Get to Level Three

Create a plantwide program.

Create guidelines for reducing inventory.

Inventory reduction is not truly effective until the entire factory gets involved. Therefore it is important to establish an inventory reduction program with deadlines and targets, in a format everyone in the plant can understand and work together on.

An inventory reduction program begins with a study of current conditions—lead time, inventory amount, process sequence, and so on. After getting an accurate measure of current inventory levels, program leaders establish their ideal level as an ultimate goal. Next, they establish intermediate goals as first and second targets and link their progress in reducing WIP with countermeasures to address various related problems.

Important Point

- Create an inventory reduction program handbook that everyone can follow.

Level Three

Start a handbook-based plantwide inventory reduction program.

At level three, the entire company is pursuing inventory reduction, using a handbook to coordinate their methods, and has achieved the intermediate target of cutting WIP in half. Inventory has been reduced within each section and also between sections so that WIP flows smoothly. Everyone understands the importance of reducing inventory, the effects it brings, and the specific methods for reaching targets.

Using handbook guidelines, teams are formed to address inventory reduction needs for specific parts. The team works through the organization to reduce inventory levels for its assigned parts.

In offices, sorting trays help reduce paperwork inventory. First, measure the typical daily amount of paperwork and establish a target amount. To make work flow more smoothly, sort paperwork into items that can be processed immediately and items that require more information. With half the paperwork, desktops will be much neater and cleaner.

Corrective Action to Get to Level Four

Reduce WIP by shortening the production line.

Reduce the number of processes.

Up through level three, the emphasis has been on reducing inventory levels within and between existing processes. To get to level four everyone must also work to reduce work-in-process by shortening the production line itself.

In assembly processes, make lots as small as possible and establish level production (load smoothing). Think of ways to consolidate the assembly line to eliminate waste. Leveling production also helps reduce the number of processing (machining) processes.

Eventually, problems related to the other 19 keys, such as defects, equipment breakdowns, and human relations issues, will also have to be addressed to enable further reduction of inventory. On the staff side, offices can redesign their operational procedures to reduce paperwork in process.

Important Points

- Implement small-lot production.
- Reduce WIP within and between processes.

Level Four

Systematize both equipment and methodology.

Reduce inventory by 75 percent.

Integrating production lines at various points has resulted in lower WIP levels, and the fewer labor-hours required eliminate operational waste. Shorter production lines enable shorter schedules. For example, in-process inventory on a press line is cut in half by combining trimming and piercing into one process that takes half the time.

Level-four factories have converted to "pull production" whereby a downstream process draws goods from the process upstream. This and further reductions in supplied parts, WIP, and labor-hours have dramatically reduced inventory. Everyone understands the connection between reduced WIP and reduced labor-hours.

At level four, many of the plant's quality and equipment breakdown problems have been identified and addressed, so new inventory reductions are less likely to disrupt production. Also, the company has implemented clerical improvements to shorten processing time.

Important Point

- The company has reached level three or higher in the other 19 keys.

Corrective Action to Get to Level Five

Unite manufacturing with sales, R&D, and suppliers in the goal of satisfying customer needs.

To get to level five, all parts of the company, and even its suppliers, must unite to create an organization that responds accurately and promptly to customer needs. This requires a lean organization that has shortened new product lead time by minimizing all types of inventory, including information.

To reach this level, various production-related imbalances must be corrected through production leveling and other problem-solving methods. The company must have strengthened its manufacturing quality to at least level four in the other 19 keys, such as by cross-training operators, establishing supplier quality support, and implementing advanced process management methods. The production line should be completely integrated and using mixed production to minimize WIP and boost flexibility.

Important Point

- Create a manufacturing system that produces only what is needed and only when it is needed.

Level Five

Change-adaptive manufacturing quality has been established.

The company is better able to ensure customer satisfaction.

With processes streamlined, the plant's material and information inventory are reduced by more than 80 percent, preparing the company to manufacture products flexibly in response to diverse customer needs. For example, assembly lines can now handle mixed lots with ease. The factory can thus adapt quickly, shipping finished products in the amount and sequence requested by the sales department.

Moreover, the company has drastically reduced lead time for order processing, new product development and design, manufacturing, and shipment, which enables it to respond better and faster to user needs.

Important Point

- The company has reached at least level four in the other 19 keys.

Key 5

Quick Changeover Technology

Taking the first step toward goal-oriented improvement and the "single changeover" challenge.

While wide-variety, small-lot production is a key ingredient for adaptability to change and improved productivity, it is also important to duplicate the advantages of large-lot production. Quick changeover technologies offer some ways to do this.

Quick changeover is not just technology; it is also a consciousness revolution that leads away from simply improving current conditions and toward goal-oriented improvement. The quick changeover challenge is an opportunity to experience and affirm the goal-oriented improvement approach of the 20 Keys program.

Quick changeover is an essential part of any production system that wants to adapt promptly to change. "Single changeover" (under ten minutes) must be achieved in setup and assembly as well as in pressing and machining processes. Companies must also carry out the clerical counterpart of quick changeover—"single file" retrieval (where anyone can find any file within one minute).

Many companies have succeeded in reducing changeover times, realizing the importance of adaptability in making good products faster and cheaper. Remember that the other 19 keys are also important to the quality of manufacturing, and work to improve their levels as well.

Level One

Lack of understanding

People mistakenly think that increasing lot sizes is a good way to reduce changeover time.

Managers and workers see changeovers as a necessary evil. They recognize that changeovers must be done to setup for different products on the line, and they accept that it takes a long time.

Managers also believe that changeovers require special skills and must be done by trained technicians, even though they would rather have the regular operators do it. To minimize time and trouble, managers in level-one factories try to increase lot sizes to have fewer changeovers.

This approach entails predicting order levels, then planning production with the largest lots possible to minimize changeovers. Naturally, this leads to large inventory levels, overproduction waste, and a higher defect rate.

Corrective Action to Get to Level Two

Understand that overproduction is a form of waste.

The level-one company must learn that overproduction not only wastes assets by creating excess warehouse inventory, it also gives rise to other kinds of waste, such as wasted motion, defect production, work-in-process, and conveyance.

Once factory managers understand that changeover can be done in less than ten minutes, they become interested in adopting quick changeover technologies.

Any factory where you hear "I wonder if we're making too many of these," or "How much is in here, anyway?" or "We're out of space!" is a factory in dire need of quick changeover improvement.

Important Point

- A need for quick changeover also arises when a company reaches level two in Key 4 (inventory reduction) or Key 8 (coupled manufacturing).

Level Two

Quick changeover studies begin

Some employees are learning how to implement single changeover.

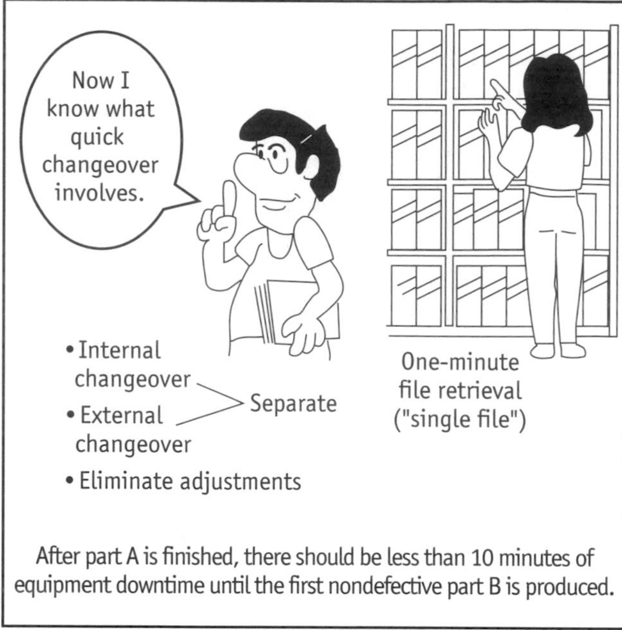

After part A is finished, there should be less than 10 minutes of equipment downtime until the first nondefective part B is produced.

Factory managers and operators now understand the need for quick changeover and have begun studying its methods. Some have already mastered single changeover methods, which include the following:

- Measuring changeover times
- Distinguishing between internal changeover (activities for which equipment must be stopped) and external changeover (activities that can be done with equipment running, such as setup and cleanup)
- Converting internal changeover to external changeover
- Changeover teamwork
- Elimination of adjustments
- Keeping equipment downtime to under 10 minutes. In offices, the goal is to retrieve documents or files from shelves or cabinets in less than one minute.

However, learning quick changeover methods and reducing changeover times on a few machines is not enough to achieve productivity improvement throughout the factory. For that, the factory needs a "consciousness revolution."

Corrective Action to Get to Level Three

Full participation of factory employees in implementing single changeover.

Getting to level three takes more than having a few people understand quick changeover methods. For better results, establish single changeover at one machine, and then have that changeover team demonstrate their methods to everyone else (companywide deployment). Specific steps involved include the following:

- Select a model machine for single changeover.
- Form a quick changeover team for that machine.
- Study how changeover is currently done.
- Draw up a changeover operation improvement sheet.
- Use the sheet to record problems and countermeasures.
- Perform a changeover on the model machine after implementing the improvements (countermeasures).

If changeover is still over 10 minutes, go back to the changeover operation improvement sheet and devise new countermeasures.

Offices can basically follow these same steps. Each department or division should exhibit its own model as a springboard for a companywide switch to single changeover.

Important Point

- Create teams for model changeovers and use changeover operation improvement sheets to record and display changeover improvements.

Level Three

Over 10 percent of changeover processes have become single changeovers.

Offices have achieved single changeover in retrieving documents and files.

At level three, the factory has a well-defined 20 Keys support organization and people are keen to establish single changeover companywide.

Single changeover has become a topic for team activities, which are full of energy and enthusiasm. At this point, just about everyone understands the key points of single changeover. At least 10 percent of all changeover is under 10 minutes, and victory cheers can be heard from changeover teams as they reach their single changeover goals.

Some offices have achieved one-minute file retrieval; others have seen its benefits and are striving to implement it too.

When a company reaches this level, we know that the goal-oriented approach has taken hold. It fuels everyone's enthusiasm for higher quality and lower costs as they pursue the other 19 keys as well.

Corrective Action to Get to Level Four

Hold quick changeover demonstrations.

Holding quick changeover demonstrations is an excellent way to propel the company toward level four. They enable successful changeover teams to show everyone how changeover can be reduced for various kinds of machines and processes.

Changeover teams should also describe and illustrate the steps they took and problems they encountered on the road to success.

Get as many equipment operators as possible to attend these demonstrations. Some corporate managers should also be there. It is very effective to have top managers recognize the team's accomplishment with an award of some kind.

These demonstrations motivate not only the teams well on their way toward single changeover but also those whose efforts are lagging behind. Ideally, the demonstrations should encourage quick changeover progress in the entire factory.

Important Points

- Use quick changeover demonstrations to build understanding and encourage broader implementation.
- Use a companywide emphasis to build motivation.

Level Four

Single changeover has been achieved on all machines currently in use.

Single file retrieval has been achieved in at least one office.

In the level-four factory, single changeover has been established and changeover exhibitions have been held for all currently used types of machines and equipment.

Likewise, at least one office has established one-minute file retrieval to locate any document on request. This is usually accomplished by having several people trained for the task, so that someone is always available to retrieve information.

Single changeover (also known as "instant changeover") should be precisely defined to suit the company's conditions, so that everyone has a clear idea of their goals. For example, it may be appropriate to hold a changeover demonstration for a certain machine as soon as single changeover is achieved for two types of parts, regardless of how many employees it takes to perform the changeover. The changeover team should not feel discouraged if they are still unable to perform single changeover for other parts, especially new product parts that are introduced later on.

Important Point

- The factory should have reached level three or higher in the other 19 keys.

Corrective Action to Get to Level Five

Any operator should be able to change over for any part in less than 10 minutes.

Manufacturing companies are always developing new products or models, so the parts manufactured must also change. Consequently, a changeover team that finally accomplishes single changeover for a certain part might learn that the part will be replaced next month by a new part with new changeover specifications. Therefore, they must develop single changeover methods that can be applied to virtually all possible parts.

A team should learn how to do a changeover within one manufacturing cycle—i.e., within the time required to process one part. That way the production line rhythm can continue smoothly, with changeover fitting into the time slot occupied by one part.

In offices, the aim is to establish one-minute file retrieval for all documents and files, new and old.

Important Points

- Work toward single changeover for any part, at any time, and by any operator.
- Strive for changeover within one processing cycle.

Level Five

Single changeover is applied to all machines and all parts.

Working toward even shorter cycle-time changeover.

The challenge at level five is to devise methods that enable even less than a full changeover crew to accomplish single changeover. This requires simplified changeover procedures and elimination of all adjustment tasks. At level five, the changeover crews have already accomplished the feat of enabling anyone, from seasoned veteran to new employee, to perform flawless changeover in under ten minutes, and with no defective goods on the first run after changeover.

The goal of single changeover for any part includes brand new parts. Likewise, the goal of cycle-time changeover means that even if the cycle is only one minute, changeover can be completed in that time.

Important Point

- The factory should have reached level four or higher in the other 19 keys.

Key 6

Manufacturing Value Analysis (Methods Improvement)

Improvements to reduce motion, increase human and mechanical efficiency, and establish better methods.

Although individual improvement suggestions are a good thing, a plantwide approach to devising and implementing improvements in methods yields even greater results. Manufacturing value analysis (MVA) analyzes the functions of individual manufacturing steps or motions and analyzes whether they add value to the product. Any motion that does not add value to the product is considered waste that should be eliminated. It is a method that effectively raises the entire factory's productivity while lowering costs.

MVA yields labor-saving improvements as well as improvements in human and mechanical efficiency. The goal of this powerful two-pronged approach is nothing less than a doubling of productivity. Moreover, MVA is concerned not only with production departments but also with clerical and other indirect departments, aiming toward companywide improvement. In reality, the direct-manufacturing departments are in many ways driven by the indirect departments.

The essential activities of MVA are making and using operations improvement sheets and improvement planning charts, all in pursuit of the main objective of doubling productivity.

Implementing Key 6 by itself would be a slow, difficult endeavor. To reach higher levels in this key, it is important also to make progress in other keys. Your company should reach at least level four in this key to double its productivity as a strong, change-adaptive manufacturer.

Level One

There is a shotgun approach to improvements.

People have little concern for improving methods.

At level-one factories, improvements come haphazardly, mainly as individual improvements via an employee suggestion system.

However, only so much can be gained by this approach, since it relies on large numbers of unrelated individual improvements rather than on a systematic approach.

Consequently, most of the suggested improvements concern ways to make particular tasks easier, such as by switching from a crescent wrench to a ratchet wrench for fastening bolts. Such an approach fails to consider the wider context of neighboring processes and the factory as a whole. Therefore these individual improvements rarely have much overall effect on manufacturing quality.

Level Two

Systematic improvement making has begun at each process.

Time values are part of a systematic, quantified approach.

At a level-two factory, improvement groups have begun to adopt more systematic methods, such as listing obstacles to improvement and applying the 5W1H method (asking who, what, when, where, why, and how). It is important to create a workplace climate that promotes systematic methods.

At level one, the climate is suspicion and antagonism toward studying current conditions and potential improvements in terms of time measurement. Workers fear that the result will be shorter standard times and more difficult, time-pressed work conditions. When implementing time studies at level two, the workers themselves should make the time measurements to determine the value of proposed improvements, since they actually perform the work and are in the best position to understand it.

Once you have created a climate in which everyone recognizes the value of systematic time measurements, people will start viewing individual improvements from the broader perspective of an entire line or plant.

Important Point

- Look at individual operations in the context of the entire process.

Problems at Level Two

Operations improvement sheets are not filled out adequately.

Key 6 involves implementing operations improvement sheets to clearly and quantitatively identify the kinds of improvements needed for an entire series of work operations, devise specific countermeasures, and keep improvements on schedule. Workplaces that need them should make operator-machine (O-M) charts as a preparatory step.

Operations improvement sheets break operations into work elements that can be analyzed to identify waste and other problems. After that, they help improvement groups plan countermeasures and estimate their effects. Operations improvement sheets also keep a clear record of who is in charge of what and the deadline for completing planned countermeasures.

Typical problems encountered by groups using operations improvement sheets include the following:

- Inability to clearly grasp the problem points.
- Lack of knowledge about how to devise good countermeasures.
- Loosely assigned responsibilities.
- Failure to set clear deadlines.

All these problems need to be resolved before you are ready to begin doubling productivity.

Level Three

People have learned how to make systematic improvements at each process.

At level three, people have learned to focus on individual work elements with a sharp eye for eliminating waste, which they now recognize as anything that does not add value to the product. They use the operations improvement sheet to distinguish between "real work" and "waste," and to analyze the various types of waste.

A level-three factory includes improvement teams that have learned to use operations improvement sheets for their improvement themes and have thereby managed to improve their work efficiency by as much as 30 percent. This systematic approach has paid off with concrete, clearly measurable effects.

Improvement teams have also learned how to identify problem points in individual work elements and how to correct them with countermeasures. They have been trained to use various industrial engineering methods to devise effective improvements, such as motion study, conveyance analysis, and process analysis.

Important Points

- Learn to identify problem points.
- Learn to devise effective countermeasures.

Problems at Level Three

Improvement-making must be carried further to raise human and mechanical efficiency.

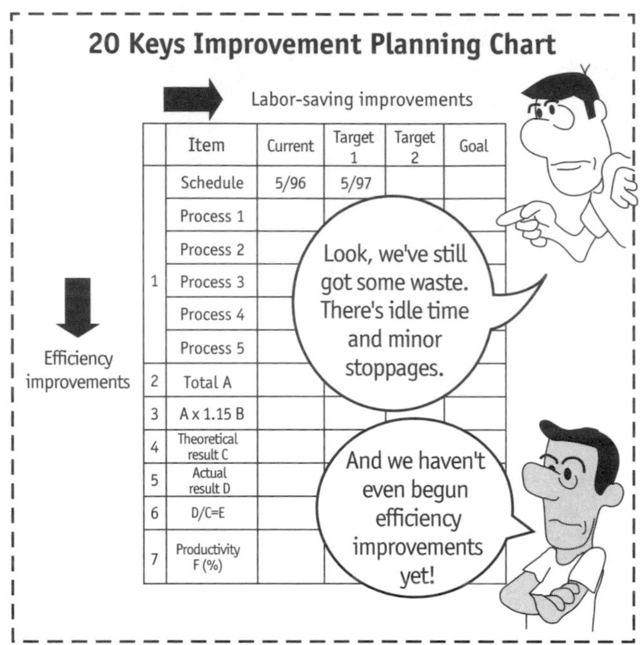

	Item	Current	Target 1	Target 2	Goal
1	Schedule	5/96	5/97		
	Process 1				
	Process 2				
	Process 3				
	Process 4				
	Process 5				
2	Total A				
3	A x 1.15 B				
4	Theoretical result C				
5	Actual result D				
6	D/C=E				
7	Productivity F (%)				

Although improvement teams have learned to use operations improvement sheets to make labor-saving improvements, they have yet to address the various kinds of waste, including idle time created by labor-saving improvements, that must be addressed by improvements in human and mechanical efficiency. The "20 Keys Improvement Planning Chart" is a form that helps teams plan both labor-saving and efficiency-boosting improvements.

When using MVA, improvement teams should plan countermeasures that have a cumulative work element time savings of about 50 percent. Specifically, this may require reducing human labor by various means while raising efficiency, such as setting up a system to automate the factory during lunch break, fully automating material handling processes, upgrading machine performance at bottleneck processes, and conducting work element analysis based on O-M charts. Raising human and mechanical efficiency in this way is a key weapon in the battle to double productivity.

Important Points

- Increase time savings until you reach the target value.
- Do not hesitate to enlist help from other departments when necessary.

Level Four

Labor-saving and efficiency-boosting improvements have enabled the factory to double its productivity.

At level four, the entire plant celebrates success at manufacturing value analysis. Waste has been eliminated from the coupling points between different types of processes and operation times have been cut in half.

People are in the habit of using the 20 Keys Improvement Planning Chart and have reached their final goal of doubling productivity in all operations. To get this far in Key 6, the factory must already have reached at least level three in the other 19 keys, since those other keys provide some of the footholds needed to reach the productivity-doubling goal. At this point, everyone has a keen sense of the synergistic effects of making improvements based on the interrelationship of the 20 Keys.

Important Point

- Reach at least level three in the other 19 keys.

Problems at Level Four

The companywide system of cooperation is still not fully stable.

After changes in production volume or product design, it takes time to bring productivity back up to its doubled level.

Having reached level four, the factory has implemented both labor-saving and efficiency improvements and has thoroughly eliminated waste from work processes, thereby doubling productivity. However, a close look will reveal that the companywide system of mutual cooperation lacks stability. Also, the factory is unable to maintain the doubled level of productivity in the wake of major changes in production volume or product design. Such changes cause productivity to drop significantly, and it takes some time to restore doubled productivity.

Taking improvement further will require cooperation with the design and R&D staff. Value engineering (VE) can help designers make new products that emphasize only genuinely needed functions. Basic researchers can assist by devising new materials that can dramatically raise productivity. Other avenues of potential improvement include adoption of the latest labor-saving equipment, such as industrial robots and FMS (flexible manufacturing systems). Computers and sensors can also save labor in certain factory management and inspection tasks.

Important Point

- As you continue making improvements, consider new labor-saving technologies.

Progress toward Automated Production

At level four, the factory has firmly established the practice of making operation improvements, which is repeated whenever necessary to keep the factory responsive even to major changes in product design or production volume.

With close cooperation between the product design staff and basic R&D staff, the level-four company is working to adopt the latest labor-saving equipment and systems, such as FMS, computer-integrated manufacturing (CIM), and strategic information systems (SIS).

Important Point

- The factory should have reached at least level four in the other 19 keys.

Level Five

The improvement-making process is systematic and is implemented repeatedly.

The manufacturing system is promptly adaptive to changes in product design and production volume.

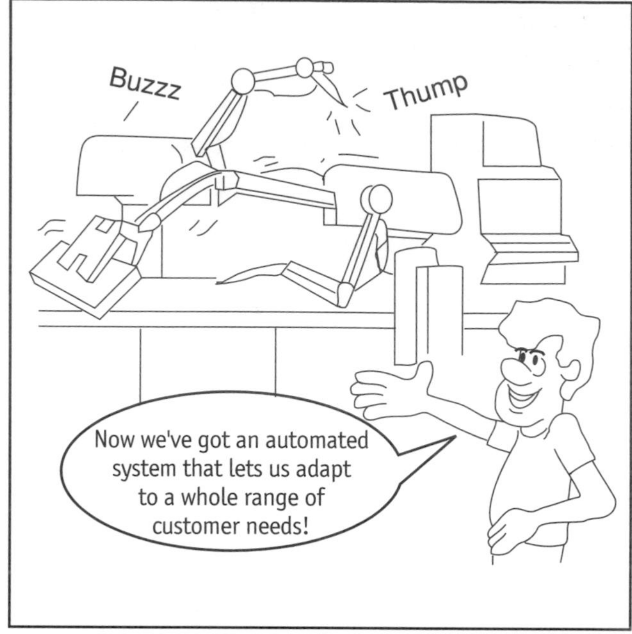

Automated manufacturing systems were popular in Japan during the high-growth era, when they were mainly designed and used for large-lot production. Transfer machines are a typical example. Such machines were useful as long as there was little variety in product models. Today, advances in LSI technology have enabled the development of newer automated equipment that can flexibly adapt to diverse user needs.

The 20 Keys Matrix Chart on the next page outlines countermeasures to take in related keys that will boost progress in Key 6. (The segment on page 69 is one column from a 20-column, 20-row matrix showing how each key supports every other key. See pages 111, 173, and 213 for three other segments of the matrix.)

20 Keys Matrix

Target Key: Key 6–Manufacturing Value Analysis (Improvement in Methods)

Countermeasures for related keys to help improve the target key.	
1. Cleaning and organizing	Eliminate awkward motions in picking up and replacing parts and tools.
2. Rationalizing the system/ management of objectives	Companywide commitment to doubling productivity and establishment of quantitative targets for specific operations.
3. Improvement teams	Use motion study in team improvement efforts.
4. Reducing inventory	Reduce inventory to reveal and remove waste from work motions and to shorten production time.
5. Quick changeover	Raise productivity by shortening changeover times and reducing labor needs.
6. Manufacturing value analysis	
7. Zero monitor manufacturing	Use "one-page standards" to eliminate procedural confusion from offices and improve efficiency.
8. Coupled manufacturing	Clarify operation links and reduce productivity loss due to idle time.
9. Maintaining equipment	Carry out effective maintenance for early prevention of breakdowns, line stoppages, etc.
10. Time control and commitment	Practice a disciplined schedule so that work can start and end on time.
11. Quality assurance system	Make improvements that work to eliminate defect production.
12. Developing your suppliers	Use in-house models to teach operation improvements; work together to plan cost reductions for purchased parts.
13. Eliminating waste (treasure map)	Hold team contests to remove waste from operations.
14. Empowering workers	Enable employees to make or modify some of their tools and equipment.
15. Skill versatility and cross-training	Implement cross-training to prevent productivity loss due to idle time, etc.
16. Production scheduling	Schedule operations to avoid idle time and prevent productivity loss.
17. Efficiency control	Use graphs to track efficiency improvements and invigorate operation.
18. Using information systems	Make good use of NC machines and other computer-controlled equipment to raise productivity.
19. Conserving energy and materials	Implement energy- and resource-saving improvements as well as time-saving improvements.
20. Leading technology/ site technology	Introduce new technologies to achieve productivity-boosting improvements.

Key 7

Zero Monitor Manufacturing

For zero defects and zero monitoring work.

Continuous unassisted automation involves not only processing workpieces but also feeding them in and extracting them. In a wide-variety, small-lot production system, automation is further complicated by the need for frequent changeovers. However, it is relatively easy to automate a one-cycle process.

In fact, one-cycle automation is a prerequisite for establishing a reliable system of multiprocess handling (one operator handling several machines or processes). When the operator leaves one machine to start working at another, the machine left behind must be able to operate without monitoring until the next cycle. If a machine can repeat the same cycle continuously without monitoring, it should be able to do so while the operator is at lunch. Further, if a one-cycle machine can operate unmonitored for more than 10 minutes during the lunch break, it can also run unmonitored after the shift.

To establish unassisted, unmonitored operation, first ask what makes it necessary for the machine to be assisted or monitored, then find ways to eliminate these factors. If an automatic machine must be stopped to clear a defective product, then the machine must be improved so that it never turns out defects. This is how a "zero monitoring" campaign also works as a "zero defects" campaign.

In assembly lines, automation requires the elimination of line imbalances that cause idle time. In clerical and other staff departments, a one-page standard for each procedure will help eliminate the "monitoring" work of having to think about it or look it up.

Level One

No one realizes that monitoring is waste, not work.

In many companies people don't understand that monitoring is not work but waste. One plant manager actually announced that "my policy is to enable everyone to monitor the machine processes." The purpose of such "work" is usually to watch out for production of defective goods. People accept the idea that automated equipment must be monitored because the machine might start cranking out rejects.

At such companies, people think it is impossible for one operator to handle more than one machine or process at once. Operators who do little but monitor their machines have the idea that the machines are doing their work for them.

In staff departments, people waste a lot of time trying to recall how a certain procedure should be done, for lack of clear and readily available instructions.

Corrective Action to Get to Level Two

Separate machine work from human work.

If a machine is working, no human should be working for it.

First of all, everyone must learn to see automatic machines as robots that can operate without supervision. They must also understand that simply watching a machine work is not work but waste—it does not add value to the product.

Considering the automatic shaping or milling processes that certain machine tools can perform, it might be appropriate to think of them as "baby robots." To become bigger and better robots, they need nurturing—such as improvements to ensure that they will automatically stop after finishing an automatic machining operation. This enables operators to leave the machine alone during operation. You cannot dramatically improve the productivity of a semi-automated factory unless the machines can be maintained and improved to operate automatically without defects.

In staff departments, using one-page standards avoids time spent on unnecessary questions and answers and also helps prevent human error.

Important Points

- Machine tools are baby robots!
- One-page standards help people get work done without having to ask or be checked by others.

Level Two

Everyone recognizes that monitoring is waste.

Understanding that monitoring is waste, not work, is not enough to relieve the operators' fear that their equipment will malfunction when they are not looking. To eliminate this risk, operators and others need to devise equipment improvements that ensure reliable unmonitored operation.

At this level everyone is learning that to eliminate monitoring you must also eliminate defect production. Start by listing all of the machines in the factory that are currently monitored as they run. Then select a machine to improve as a model for unassisted, unmonitored operation.

In offices, draft or select a one-page standard form and make two lists of work processes: routine work and non-routine work. Then start writing one-page standards for the routine work. Once you show how to make routine work simpler and easier with a one-page standard, people will understand the advantages of using them. In assembly work, one-page standards help eliminate line stoppages due to line imbalances.

Corrective Action to Get to Level Three

Establish one-cycle unmonitored operation during the lunch break.

Get everyone involved in developing unmonitored operation.

The improvement effort should begin with establishing one-cycle unmonitored operation during the lunch break. Once you have succeeded at that, you know that the machine is capable of one-cycle unmonitored operation at other times. To start, devise ways to eliminate defect production, then make improvements to ensure that the machine will automatically stop after each cycle. If the same cycle can be repeated consecutively for a lot of workpieces, one-cycle unmonitored operation will make a big difference in productivity.

Everyone should be acutely aware that monitoring is waste and should be involved in efforts to develop unmonitored operation. These efforts will go better if people work in teams rather than individually. Managers can support these efforts by determining when one-cycle unmonitored operation is needed as a step toward more difficult continuous unmonitored operation.

Important Points

- Take measures to ensure that the machine will not produce rejects.
- Correct imbalances in assembly lines to eliminate idle-time waste.
- Make operator-machine (O-M) charts to eliminate idle time in machine and human work.

Level Three

At least 10 percent of the projects have succeeded in establishing unmonitored one-cycle operation during the lunch break.

At least 10 percent of office operations have one-page standards.

The level-three factory has established unmonitored operation for at least 10 percent of the equipment. During lunch, some machines can operate on their own for only a few minutes while others can operate automatically for the entire lunch break. You may overhear operators boasting about how their machines are working while they're eating, although others have not reached that point yet. Everyone is now deeply concerned with the need for unmonitored operation. Some operators have learned to use O-M charts to study operator and machine work and reduce idle time.

Key 5 (quick changeover technology) focused on consistently producing non-defective first-run goods as a prerequisite for single changeover. From a Key 7 perspective, a machine for which single changeover has been achieved is a machine that is ready for unmonitored operation.

In this way, the factory gradually takes on a new atmosphere that encourages elimination of equipment monitoring by spreading examples of successful unmonitored one-cycle operation throughout the factory.

Staff departments now have one-page standards for at least 10 percent of the work procedures, which has helped people share their expertise and cross-train. The one-page standards also are the basis for creating operation improvement sheets in efforts to improve work procedures.

Corrective Action to Get to Level Four

Establish unmonitored lunchtime operation for all machines.

As more people learn how others have established one-cycle unmonitored operation, soon it will be possible to run virtually all machines automatically during the lunch break.

As part of these efforts, operators and improvement teams will focus on machines that are still not reliable enough to operate without monitoring. If even one machine in a line produces defective goods or breaks down unpredictably, the line cannot operate automatically without monitoring, even for one cycle. Therefore, everyone must work together to improve unreliable equipment.

Machines that can operate unmonitored for at least 10 minutes during lunch should be considered candidates for after-hours operation as well. To enable this, the equipment must be fitted with an auto-stop mechanism that cuts off electric power or air supply when the desired operation is finished. There should also be an automated operation switch to set the machine for unmonitored operation during the lunch break or after the shift.

Level Four

All machines can operate during lunch without monitoring and many operators can handle two or more machines.

Operators are working on after-hours unmonitored operation.

One-page standards have been prepared for all office operations.

At level four, all machines are automated for at least one cycle during the lunch hour. Machines are equipped to sound an alarm when the cycle is up, and the machine shuts down automatically if no one responds to set up the machine for the next cycle. Thus all machines are able to operate reliably (without producing rejects) for a certain period with no monitoring.

When machines have reached this state, they are ready for unmonitored automatic operation after work hours. However, if the machines are operating after their handlers have gone for the day, you must consider the problem of chips and shavings that will pile up. These problems are dealt with in Keys 1 (the 4Ss) and 10 (time control and commitment). When the equipment has been improved to the point where reliable unmonitored operation is possible, operators will have more time available and can handle several machines without worrying about breakdowns or rejects.

Level-four offices have fully implemented one-page standards, which has helped office workers learn new skills, further improve operations, and work more efficiently. Now even substitute employees can function without making mistakes.

Corrective Action to Get to Level Five

Use O-M charts to identify idle time.

Work independently and enthusiastically to devise measures for eliminating every second of idle time or monitoring time.

When operators are wondering what to do with their spare time, the factory is at level four, not level five. To get to level five, the frontline operators must get actively involved in identifying idle time and seeking productive things to do with it.

O-M charts can be used to clearly identify every second of idle time and to suggest ways to shorten cycle times. The key point is to try to find useful work to do during the idle time.

These efforts also depend on training to give operators the technical knowledge they need to devise and implement the corrective action that leads to level five.

Level Five

The factory now has almost zero monitoring time.

The firmly established zero-monitoring campaign is also a zero-defects campaign.

The level-five factory has all machines operating automatically and without monitoring for at least one cycle. Operators can each handle several machines and some operators even have an occasional moment to lend a hand at neighboring processes or lines. They are all comfortable with their multiprocess routine.

Some painting/coating factories have individual operators achieving the work that used to require four operators, freeing employees to work productively at other tasks. Some have almost totally eliminated monitoring time.

In level-five factories, the operators have been personally involved in developing a comfortable work rhythm that includes virtually zero idle time.

On assembly lines, various improvements have rid the line of imbalances to produce a smooth flow of operations.

In offices and staff departments, implementation of one-page standards includes even nonroutine procedures. Consequently staff productivity is at an all-time high, with better skills training and efficiency control to boot. Office employees have also learned how to make regular improvements in their one-page standards. As in the manufacturing departments, they too have eliminated monitoring in a way that also helps ensure zero defects.

Key 8

Coupled Manufacturing

Building cooperative ties between neighboring processes.

Although some factories have responded to the diversification of customer needs by shifting to wide-variety, small-lot production, other manufacturers mistakenly rely on large inventories for product diversity. Organizational rigidity is behind much of this stockpiling. Some companies have built such thick "walls" between departments and divisions that the cost of reorganizing would be immense. Indeed, tearing down organizational walls to allow goods and information to flow laterally through the company is likely to uncover problems and obstacles. However, manufacturing companies must create an organization in which departments can cooperate closely, for this alone will help make the company quickly adaptive to change.

Production lines should set up "stores" between processes so the operator from the following process "goes shopping" there for inventory items. Everyone must see the next process as the customer. Each process must provide quality products in the desired amounts to their store so their next-process customer can get exactly what is needed next. This is called "pull" production.

Some companies may work better with a "push" system in which the production schedule determines how many products each process will turn out and send to the next process. At the next process, operators must keep busy to use up the delivered inventory.

In both systems, inventory levels for the next process are made highly visible. Staff departments break down barriers to smooth flow of information, such as by adopting the fishbowl discussion method, a radical new concept that changes the workplace from a collection of semi-autonomous groups into an integrated, smoothly functioning whole.

Level One

Each section does its own thing

Each workplace functions independently.

At a level-one company, the organizational structure is clear: different workplaces compete in producing good results and people are concerned only with how well their own workplace is doing. Welders, machinists, and other workers are concerned only with their own work, looking for the easiest way to get their work done to meet the production schedule.

For example, when a workshop receives its production schedule for the month, the employees check the parts quantities needed that month and then begin making all of the Part A requirement, then all of Part B, and so on. They don't consider what sequence of production would best serve the next process. Instead, they choose the large-lot approach as the most convenient approach for themselves.

Often in this situation there is no place to store the large lots between processes. The transport staff are unlikely to get much help from employees at the next process, who are also thinking only of their own work.

Naturally, such a system makes it hard for downstream processes to meet their own production schedules in an orderly manner, since they have little control over their supply of materials and parts. This kind of system also tends to result in huge piles of inventory between processes.

Corrective Action to Get to Level Two

Observe how inventory piles up between processes.

When you study how inventory (goods or information) piles up in factories or offices, you will notice that upstream processes are turning it out according to their own schedules, while downstream processes are still hard put to find what they need for their own scheduled work. Moreover, the location for storing the inventory is poorly communicated, so downstream employees must sometimes go looking for it.

With each workgroup concerned only about itself, there is little understanding or cooperation between processes. This situation must be remedied.

The basic concept behind coupling manufacturing processes is that neighboring processes must communicate with each other to reach an understanding about inventory and where it is to be stored. The object is to make needed inventory readily available to the next process in a clearly visible way. To do this, you must establish smoothly functioning connections between processes.

Important Points

- Coordinate smooth communication and connections between processes.
- Keep all inventory between two processes in the same place.
- Find ways to reduce the amount of inventory between processes.

Level Two

Emphasize the connections between processes and full employee participation in improvement making.

There are various ways to improve connections between processes, and the most appropriate way depends on the type of product and how it is made, or the type of information and how it flows. The first step is to get everyone involved in studying possible ways and selecting the best one for the situation. Employees at each process must learn the importance of creating smooth connections between processes so that they will take these studies seriously.

For example, one method calls for inventory to be organized like supermarkets, with items placed neatly on well-marked shelves. Another method uses special inventory control pallets for establishing interprocess connections.

Corrective Action to Get to Level Three

After establishing the type of connection to use, have leaders of neighboring processes meet to work out the details.

In offices, hold meetings to explain the fishbowl discussion approach.

Various approaches exist for connecting departments and improving the flow of inventory between their workers, whether the inventory is goods or information. Options include the supermarket approach, inventory pallets, and kanban cards. Whatever method is selected, the leaders of the two employee groups must meet to work out how to smooth out the interprocess connection.

Since the next process is the customer, the leader of the previous process is basically responsible for setting up a system that makes it easy for the next process to receive inventory. The leader of the next process generally suggests the particular method to be used.

To smooth the flow of information between processes, start by meeting to explain the fishbowl discussion method. This approach structures the discussion of hot issues, allowing both groups to look at each other's needs and consider each other's proposed methods to arrive at the optimal solution. (See Appendix A for a description of how it works.)

Important Point

- Plan interprocess connections (stores) that promote mutual understanding of the needs of each process.

Level Three

Factory employees begin setting up interprocess stores.

At level three, everyone is familiar with process connection approaches and has set up actual stores. Some factories can use the same kind of store everywhere, but this may not be possible when some lines manufacture large lots of similar items and other lines receive an unpredictable assortment of product orders or custom-produce individual products. The idea is to use whatever works best for each situation. The left part of the drawing shows a store placed at the end of a large-lot production line. The top number on the store sign shows the minimum inventory level, at which the production line should replenish the store. The bottom number shows the maximum level, at which production should be stopped until inventory is reduced. This system helps ensure smooth coordination with the next process. The right side of the drawing shows a control board system for production plan control of previous processes.

In offices, the fishbowl discussion method ensures that connected processes understand each other and can set up an effective store for documents and other information that flows between them.

Important Points

- Make coupling points between processes as visible as possible.
- Keep working toward companywide integration.

Corrective Action to Get to Level Four

Minimize inventory retention points so that connections between processes are automatically smooth.

Hold follow-up fish-bowl discussions two or three times a year.

Once coupling points between processes are operating smoothly, the process group leaders begin to appreciate how much easier their work has become and leaders at processes that don't have stores start to notice. Soon, everyone catches on to the store concept and eventually the entire factory starts to benefit from smoother interprocess connections.

At this point, the factory may be ready to get rid of parts warehouses between manufacturing and the assembly lines. Such warehouses hold a lot of inventory and cost time and money to manage. Before it can go, however, the parts manufacturing line and assembly line have to be smoothly coordinated using the same production rhythm. Diligent improvement efforts are needed to establish such a smooth connection.

In offices, once the fishbowl method is established, it can be used two or three times a year to plan further improvements and affirm mutual understanding.

Important Points

- Clearly display the operating rules for the inventory stores.
- Use complete, smoothly functioning inventory stores as models for training others to operate their own stores.

Level Four

Clearly visible coupling points have been established throughout the factory.

Offices are seeing positive results from the fishbowl method.

At level four, stores or other coupling points have been established between each pair of processes and the rules for operating the store are clearly posted. For example, if the supermarket method is used, employees from the next process must be able to find what they need at any time. If the special-order method is used, a control board makes the schedule clear to everyone; specially ordered products are made and delivered as scheduled, just like getting a suit made to order at a tailor.

When special rush jobs come through, the store should function as efficiently as a good restaurant in serving the order quickly to satisfy the customer.

In level-four offices, employees have begun to enjoy the effects of their fishbowl discussions—smoothly flowing information and communication.

Corrective Action to Get to Level Five

Start eliminating unnecessary coupling points.

Hold ad-hoc fishbowl meetings.

Now that the current system of stores or other coupling points is running smoothly throughout the plant, with inventory levels regularly checked at each store, it is time to work on reducing inventory. There are many benefits to be gained by this, but the improvements will require everyone's help.

Begin by studying the functions of processes and lines throughout the factory. Look for cases where functions overlap or are widely separated and try to create a more efficient factory layout.

Such a layout will involve eliminating some stores and combining lines or processes in ways that enable an overall reduction in inventory. The ultimate goal is zero inventory.

Important Points

- Reduce the amount of inventory in each store.
- Combine processes or lines.

Level Five

Plantwide integration

All interdepartmental walls have been demolished so that goods and information can flow freely.

A change-adaptive factory has been created.

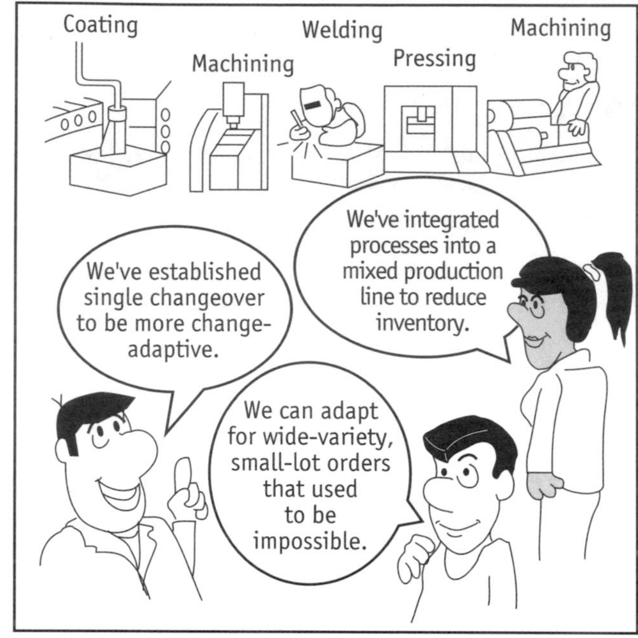

Thanks to the coupling methods and fishbowl discussion approach described earlier, the company has rid itself of the waste created by interdepartmental walls. Production periods have been shortened and costs are now much lower. A careful study of the factory's functions led to the creation of an optimum factory layout with smoother operations and much less waste.

Factory inventory has been drastically reduced by eliminating unnecessary coupling points and integrating processes into mixed production lines. These achievements, plus the establishment of single changeover, have created a wide-variety, small-lot manufacturing organization that can adapt quickly to change.

Key 9

Maintaining Equipment

Better equipment maintenance brings a higher operating rate.

When factory workers and managers use equipment without properly maintaining it ("we're too busy for that," they say), they eventually run into a bigger problem: breakdowns and line stoppages. To prevent breakdowns, you must eliminate the three evils of (1) contamination, (2) inadequate lubrication, and (3) misoperation. For best results, get everyone involved in removing these causes of equipment breakdowns.

In addition, factory workers and managers should understand the practice of preventive maintenance (PM) so they can support maintenance efforts to identify and fix minor problems in critical equipment before they cause breakdowns. A thorough maintenance management system requires the cooperation of equipment operators, who can promote PM on their equipment by checking equipment conditions against a check sheet provided by the maintenance technicians.

The 20 Keys approach involves prevention at many levels: preventing breakdowns not only for equipment in its prime but also for newly installed equipment and older equipment. The benefits to be gained include zero breakdowns and far fewer minor stoppages due to quality problems, material shortages, or changeover delays. You can greatly increase the equipment's operating rate, which translates to higher productivity and lower production costs.

Level One

Run the machines into the ground.

At level-one factories, production personnel typically use machines until they break. Thinking that their only responsibility is to turn out products, operators leave all equipment maintenance to the maintenance technicians.

In such plants, production people feel they are too busy to turn over equipment for inspection, and shoo away the maintenance technicians. Maintenance staff even have trouble getting operators to use check sheets for preventive maintenance. Little wonder that level-one factories have breakdowns left and right, usually at the worst possible time for production. Then operators are up in arms, yelling for a mechanic to come quickly lest they fall behind.

The maintenance and repair system at level-one factories is inadequate in many respects. If there are any PM-trained mechanics, their morale is dampened by a lack of cooperation from equipment operators in carrying out routine checks. Communication between PM staff and operators is poor, and operators complain that the mechanics are too slow in responding to breakdowns.

In addition, level-one factories rarely bother to train equipment operators in PM methods and tend to have poorly organized maintenance programs. Odds are that several technicians share responsibility for all equipment. So when servicing a machine they have to check the maintenance log to see what has been done recently, and the maintenance log is usually not very explicit.

Corrective Action to Get to Level Two

Start PM study groups.

Make sure everyone understands the need for a maintenance management system.

The first steps are to understand why PM is needed, to study its principles, and to establish a PM program. It is easy to see how sudden malfunctions or breakdowns in key equipment can delay production or produce rejects. When operators see clearly how equipment maintenance can affect the company's success, they will understand why PM is critical.

PM is chiefly a matter of identifying and repairing equipment problems before they cause breakdowns. This involves daily inspection by operators as well as periodic inspection and servicing by maintenance technicians. The first step in setting up a maintenance management system is to create a maintenance log for every machine. Next, determine which machines are most important and most in need of PM and label these machines "designated PM equipment." Then start implementing PM measures for this equipment.

Make a PM check sheet for each designated PM machine and teach operators how to use it for daily inspection. The technicians use the same check sheets for periodic inspection and service. The initial goal is to prevent unexpected failures in all designated PM equipment.

Important Point

- Make maintenance logs for every machine in the factory.

Level Two

Everyone understands the need for PM.

PM has been implemented for the most important machines.

At level two, factories have already implemented these items:

1. Frontline workers understand the need for PM and grasp its basic principles.
2. An equipment maintenance organization has been formed.
3. A sign on each machine tells who is responsible for its maintenance.
4. Each machine has a maintenance log.
5. Important machines are labeled "Designated PM Equipment" and have first priority in efforts to eliminate breakdowns.
6. Each designated PM equipment unit has a check sheet used by the operator for daily inspection and by the maintenance technician for periodic maintenance and service.

Important Point

- Work toward zero sudden breakdowns.

Corrective Action to Get to Level Three

Get all factory employees involved in PM.

Generally, the people who use equipment are the first ones to notice equipment malfunctions and breakdowns. They know the equipment and therefore are best able to detect when something is odd and needs attention. Operators should adopt their machines as they would adopt a child and abandon the idea that inspection and maintenance is the maintenance department's job.

1. *Eliminate the three evils (contamination, inadequate lubrication, and misoperation).* Mechanics responding to equipment malfunctions should identify the cause and indicate whether it is one of the three evils. If so, the operator and manager responsible for the equipment should be told so they can plan appropriate countermeasures.
2. *Make PM a topic for improvement team activities.* Eliminating the three evils makes a good team project. It's an effort that requires specific targets and incremental improvements. Working on PM projects is also a good way to strengthen communication, inspire important discussions, and raise team morale.
3. *Make needed consumables and spare parts readily available.* Consumables and spare parts should be stored in a clearly marked location where they can be retrieved easily when needed.

Level Three

Operators know they must keep their machines in good condition and eliminate the three evils.

Level-three factories meet the following conditions:

1. Operators know they have primary responsibility for taking care of the machines they use.
2. Consumables, spare parts, and maintenance tools are kept nearby in clearly marked places to facilitate maintenance and speedy response to breakdowns.
3. Inspection and maintenance follow a set routine, and operators use occasional spare time to clean and touch up their machines.
4. The right kind of lubricant is kept on hand and operators follow clear instructions for lubricating their machines and replacing worn parts.
5. Operators are well trained to understand their machine's functions and no longer have breakdowns from mishandling.
6. In fact, there are no breakdowns caused by any of the three evils.
7. Teams have adopted maintenance improvement as a project.

Important Point

- Make eliminating the three evils (contamination, inadequate lubrication, and misoperation) a topic for team activities.

Corrective Action to Get to Level Four

Study focused improvement techniques

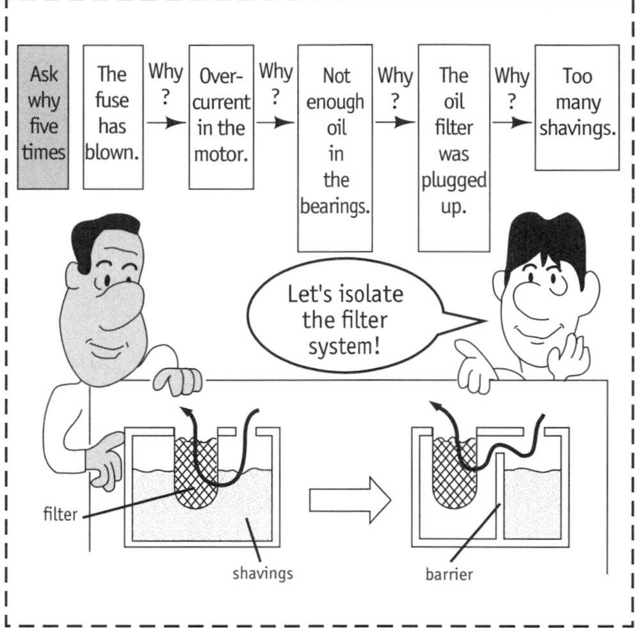

By thoroughly implementing equipment improvement management and focused improvement, a factory can reach zero breakdowns. The plant got to level three by eliminating the causes of sudden breakdowns during stable operation. However, this is not enough to prevent breakdowns that occur when commissioning new equipment or running old, worn equipment. For that, you need focused improvement.

Focused improvement is an approach that seeks to fully establish the conditions needed to prevent breakdowns. This approach starts by asking "why?" repeatedly to discover root causes of breakdowns so that problems can be fixed at the source.

Lack of stable precision in machinery is also a major cause of defects. For example, a key requirement for single changeover is that equipment must operate in a consistent manner. If a machine tool is used to process a cycle of workpieces A, B, and C, when the operator goes back to type A, it should come out exactly like the previous type A, without requiring adjustments. This is not possible when the machine tool is wobbly or otherwise inconsistent. Focused improvement must be implemented to establish reliable precision.

Important Point

- When a certain type of breakdown occurs, take steps to prevent its recurrence.

Level Four

Everyone understands and is committed to focused improvement.

The focused improvement approach is being implemented in pursuit of the zero-breakdown goal.

A level-four factory meets all of the following conditions.

1. Factory employees are studying focused improvement.
2. Tool precision is maintained to prevent defect production.
3. Measurements are taken to track equipment deterioration and prevent related problems.
4. An organization has been established for executing the PM cycle.
5. The operating rate has been raised (thanks in part to a 75 percent reduction in downtime due to minor line stoppages).
6. The factory has reached level three or higher in the other 19 keys.
7. There are no minor line stoppages caused by equipment malfunctions.

Important Points

- Raise the operating rate (reduce downtime by 75 percent).
- Reach at least level three in the other 19 keys.

Corrective Action to Get to Level Five

Use equipment that has benefited from focused improvement as teaching models.

Although focused improvement often requires specialized knowledge and skills regarding the target equipment, operators should still be involved since they are the ones who work with the equipment all the time. The operators' involvement in eliminating the three evils has made them even more knowledgeable and concerned about the condition of their machines, and they have a new perspective on their equipment's mechanisms and performance characteristics. This has equipped them to be useful partners in implementing focused improvement.

Operators who have advanced this far should be given opportunities to further increase their focused improvement knowledge and skills. Post "Focused Improvement Completed" signs on equipment that has been improved. Focused improvement needs to permeate the factory and be managed comprehensively as part of the effort to promote effective equipment management.

A company must reach at least level four in the other 19 keys to establish the footholds it needs to climb to level five.

Important Points

- Make sure operators have focused improvement skills.
- Make sure the plant has reached at least level four in the other keys.

Level Five

A focused equipment improvement program is deployed and monitored factorywide.

The overall equipment operating rate is 95 percent or higher.

The level-five factory meets all of the following conditions.

1. Most operators are proficient at focused improvement.
2. Focused improvements have made some machines better than new and have eliminated defect production.
3. Machines produce only nondefective goods in the first run after each changeover.
4. A focused improvement program has been thoroughly implemented and improvements have been implemented on all machines.
5. Follow-up management has also been thoroughly implemented and PM has been carried out on all machines.
6. The factory's PM organization is functioning smoothly and effectively.
7. The factory has reached at least level four in the other 19 keys.
8. The overall equipment operating rate is 95 percent or higher.

Key 10

Time Control and Commitment

No matter what policies a company establishes and implements in pursuit of stronger manufacturing quality and higher productivity, the result will be disappointing unless the company also has thoroughly implemented time control policies. By the same token, policies that are established but not enforced will not be improved by any amount of revision. Time policies should reflect the firm intentions of managers and supervisors and should be positively supported by frontline workers.

Workfloor time policies are the essential first step toward revolutionizing manufacturing quality: only when time policies are established and enforced can a manufacturing quality revolution truly take hold. This key is one of the hardest to implement, because it deals with attitudes as much as it does with policies. The enthusiasm generated by successful implementation of the other keys will make it possible to implement this key also.

The success of a time control policy depends on how well it fits into the framework of other policies in the organization. One factory had a problem with workers taking frequent unscheduled personal breaks. In response, management instituted a policy that included two 10-minute breaks per day, at scheduled times. Soon, however, workers were starting their breaks early and returning late, complaining that 10 minutes was too short. The new break policy didn't produce the desired result because it didn't address the reasons behind the frequent breaks.

Level One

Work and break times are left to the workers' discretion.

I visited a factory during the official lunch break (noon to 1:00 p.m.), and saw that the workers had returned to work well before 1:00. I also noticed that at 3:00 p.m. (an hour before official quitting time), people were heading for the showers already. When I asked the company president about this, he said, "Our official working hours are from 8:00 to 4:00, but we let our employees adjust the hours as it suits them. When I come to work at 7:30 a.m., there are many people already at work."

This factory had no bells or whistles to mark the start and end of the work day, and no one seemed concerned about keeping to the official hours. Any factory that operates under such conditions is a level-one factory.

Other symptoms of the level-one factory include a lack of morning meetings to start the day, no uniforms or dress code, and allowing workers to smoke on the job. It is also a bad sign when workers walk around with their hands in their pockets or when they leave room lights on unnecessarily.

Level Two

Morning "pep talk" meetings are held every day.

Morning meetings are not elaborate affairs; the idea is to gather everyone briefly for instruction and encouragement from the supervisor or manager and to energize everyone for the day's work with a group yell or cheer, like a sports team. For simplicity's sake, start with one meeting for the whole factory or for entire departments within the factory.

It is also useful to assemble briefly to kick off the after-lunch stretch, and in Japan many plants have found it effective to have a formal conclusion to the work day as well.

Level-two factories have conditions like these:

- A whistle or bell marks the start and end of work shifts.
- The morning meeting ends with a rousing cheer to get everyone going.
- The morning meeting includes some stretching or exercises to clear mental cobwebs.
- No one smokes on the job and unneeded lights are turned out during lunch.
- Workers wear uniforms or other neatly kept clothing, with name tags or patches. All safety gear is worn as prescribed.
- Employees work purposefully and energetically.

Problems at Level Two

Lack of enthusiasm during exercises and frequent tardiness at morning meetings.

In the level-two factory, morning meetings are held when the whistle blows to mark the start of the work day, but some people show up late or out of breath. Likewise, people line up at the cafeteria door (or otherwise away from their stations) even before the lunch whistle blows. One or two people doing this wouldn't be so bad if it didn't start a trend that is eventually followed by just about everyone.

At level-two factories, some workers habitually knock off 10 minutes early so they can wash up, change clothes, and be out the door when the whistle blows. Some who are rushing at quitting time don't bother to tidy up or put away their tools.

In some sections or work teams, a supervisor keeps workers disciplined, but "when the cat's away, the mice will play." Unless a supervisor is holding them back, workers who see a few others lined up for lunch before the whistle blows are likely to join the early birds to get a good place in line. When such behavioral trends are allowed to develop, there is little hope for improving time control and commitment now or in the future.

Level Three

Supervisors meet to work out time control issues.

When a factory has been at level two for several years, the conditions at that level have become habitual and it is much more difficult to make the changes needed to get to level three or four.

To overcome this inertia, supervisors from the entire factory meet and plan consistent, plantwide improvement and time control enforcement so that everyone can move forward in unison.

Level-three factories meet all of the following conditions:

- Supervisors from throughout the factory meet to discuss and coordinate time control policies.
- Workers arrive on time for morning meetings and begin work directly afterward.
- Workers do not leave their stations until the break whistle blows.
- Everyone returns tools to their proper places before leaving work. Office workers leave desktops tidy at the end of the day.
- Employees do not litter. Walkways are free of litter and dirt.
- Workers are provided with written or spoken job instructions so they are never left without something to do.

Problems at Level Three

People take their time getting to work after the morning meeting and start preparing to leave before the whistle.

At level three, you must deal with a "take it easy" attitude or valuable time will be wasted after the morning meeting and just before quitting time.

In offices, similar attitudes may exist: After the morning meeting, some workers may take quite a while sorting through their incoming paperwork tray to organize the day's work.

Such inefficient uses of starting time can be expected in plants where supervisors give frontline workers verbal directions or a scribbled note of instructions, or when they simply assume the workers know what to do next.

Level Four

Workers are conscientious about sticking to the work throughout the designated working hours.

Clearly post today's and tomorrow's work assignments in the workplace. An assignment board enables everyone, even passersby, to understand what is happening at that workplace. It also gives the workers some extra motivation to get the posted work done. This new level of conscientiousness among workplace employees also helps support the development of a new, good habit: setting up for tomorrow's work before leaving work today.

Level-four factories have the following conditions:

- Employees arrive at morning meetings on time and dressed for work.
- Morning meetings begin with exercises or stretching and end before the starting whistle.
- People do not quit working until after the end-of-day whistle blows.
- Everyone sets up for the next day's work before going home.
- Before employees leave, the supervisor posts the next day's work assignments, along with two days' notice regarding vacations. Last-minute phoned-in absences are discouraged.
- Office workers avoid long or irrelevant phone conversations. Meetings are focused and are concluded within the designated time.
- Communication (reporting, passing information, and advising) is carried out reliably and consistently.
- Managers and workers speak clearly, plainly, and courteously.

Problems at Level Four

Wasteful motions still exist among work-time activities.

Even at level-four factories, some of the work may be wasteful motion that adds nothing to the value of the product.

To become a level-five factory, workers must be able to start the next task right after finishing the last one, so that there is a steady flow of work being done. This is not possible when some of the work is physically exhausting. Therefore, fatigue-causing methods must be eliminated. This is only possible if the factory is also working on the other 19 keys. When this is accomplished, though, the factory will hum with a smooth and efficient work rhythm.

Employees at level-four factories are over the bad habit of impromptu breaks and have acquired the good habit of staying on the job except during designated breaks.

Level Five

Work is easier when it follows a steady rhythm.

By the time a factory reaches level five in Key 10, it has attained at least level four in the other 19 keys. The factory has thereby transformed itself into a revolutionized workplace staffed by energetic, highly motivated people. The cleanliness and orderliness of each workplace and the comfortable, confident smiles of the employees teach that even strict time control policies can fit smoothly and harmoniously into the rhythm of work operations.

Level-five factories meet all of the following conditions:

- Employees are performing value-adding work as soon as the starting whistle blows.
- Employees continue to perform value-adding work until the break or end-of-day whistle blows.
- Improvements have been made to eliminate all physically fatiguing work.
- Work operations have a steady rhythm that helps employees enjoy working smoothly and efficiently.
- A "first bell" sounds to remind everyone that the break is about to end.
- The factory has reached at least level four in the other 19 keys, an achievement that lends vital support to improving time control policies.

Level Five

(continued)

Employees are performing value-adding work as soon as the start whistle blows.

The chart on the next page shows how activities in the other 19 keys support progress in Key 10.

20 Keys Matrix

Target Key: Key 10–Time Control and Commitment

Countermeasures for related keys to help improve the target key.	
1. Cleaning and organizing	Keep cleaning equipment nearby to clean up messes as soon as they occur.
2. Rationalizing the system/ management of objectives	The managers take the initiative in making improvements to establish better time control policies.
3. Improvement teams	The improvement and enforcement of workfloor time policies make good topics/team activities.
4. Reducing inventory	Eliminate unneeded inventory and eliminate the need for meetings. Arrange inventory storage.
5. Quick changeover	Establish fast, precise changeover routines that leave no time for idle talking.
6. Manufacturing value analysis	Pursue an improvement plan which includes improvements that enable immediate startup after the morning meeting.
7. Zero monitor manufacturing	Set work instructions that keep employees productive at all times.
8. Coupled manufacturing	Establish smooth operation links to avoid confusion at previous and next processes.
9. Maintaining equipment	Eliminate breakdowns to enable workers to remain productive all day.
10. Time control and commitment	
11. Quality assurance system	Reduce defects, reduce the number of countermeasures needed, and reduce time spent talking.
12. Developing your suppliers	Provide guidance to suppliers by demonstrating what your factory has gained by adhering to time control policies.
13. Eliminating waste (treasure map)	Use the "treasure map" method to identify and eliminate causes of long, inefficient business talks.
14. Empowering workers	Make work assignment boards and other simple devices to help enforce workfloor time policies.
15. Skill versatility and cross-training	Cross-training and an atmosphere of mutual assistance help to harmoniously enforce time control policies.
16. Production scheduling	Establish clear sequences of operations to avoid having to stop work to discuss the next step.
17. Efficiency control	Help boost motivation by using graphs to track efficiency improvements due to enforced time control policies.
18. Using information systems	Use computer programs to help manage work efficiency and to speed up clerical processing.
19. Conserving energy and materials	Implement energy- and resource-saving improvements as part of everyone's daily activities.
20. Leading technology/ site technology	Help employees learn new skills and technologies to improve themselves and develop new abilities.

Key 11

Quality Assurance System

Building a stronger, defect-free quality assurance system.

The quality assurance (QA) system is often cited as a key ingredient for successful management in view of its direct relationship to many management objectives. QA improvement requires progress in many areas, including reducing equipment breakdowns, improving changeover speed and reliability, and invigorating team activities. The 20 Keys approach focuses improvement efforts on all of these areas and is therefore well-suited as a method for building a stronger QA system.

Unfortunately, many companies depend on inspection as the cornerstone of QA. But even the best inspection won't prevent the production of defective goods. On the contrary, a strong inspection system fosters complacency, leading to even greater defect production.

Building an effective QA system brings up various issues and shifts in emphasis, such as the change from defect discovery to defect prevention, or from work requiring sharp attention to avoid defects to work that is defect-free even when the operator is not paying attention, or from achieving "zero customer complaints" to "zero next process complaints." As we manage these shifts, we create manufacturing processes that no longer produce defective goods.

In many plants, the "defect rate" used as the main benchmark of product quality includes only rejects so defective that they must be scrapped; minor defects requiring rework are not counted. The 20 Keys approach uses an "abnormality rate" that accounts for each defect too minor for scrapping but correctable through rework. Since it is higher than the defect rate, the abnormality rate motivates improvement.

Level One

QA is left to the inspectors.

At level-one factories, people think that production is everything—they are not as concerned with the number of rejects they produce as with whether they can meet the production deadline with quality goods. They depend on their inspection system to weed out the defective products. The prevalent attitude among operators at such factories is that it's their job to make things and the inspector's job to catch mistakes. Consequently, operators are rarely held accountable for rejects produced at their stations.

This is partly because operators cannot easily tell when a product they have made is defective. Moreover, operators cannot take the time and trouble to determine causes of defects and devise countermeasures.

Instead, defect-related problems are identified later in the inspection stage, and quality control staff—consisting mainly of production engineers rather than operators—are charged with addressing the underlying causes. This detachment from frontline workers leads to ineffective countermeasures that typically fail to dramatically reduce defects.

Corrective Action to Get to Level Two

Thoroughly establish the idea that the next process is the customer and it is wrong to pass on defects.

Most factory workers believe that what they make will eventually be used; they try to be productive by making as much product as they can. To get to level two, however, the factory must inform its equipment operators whenever they produce defective goods. One way to do this is by including only nondefective goods in each operator's production volume total, so that the number of defects is duly reflected.

At the final annealing station in one casting plant, defective products were stacked in a specific place. Products with surface defects were labeled with a note saying, "I've got a skin problem," while those with shrinkage problems were marked, "I'm all lumpy." These and other entertaining devices can be used to help keep operators at the previous process more aware of defect production.

It is also a good idea to keep a daily log in which the operator at each process can record daily comments from the next process about the products the operator made the day before.

Important Point

- Do not include rejects in the production volume.

Level Two

Equipment operators inspect their own products.

One problem with having inspections at the end of a production line is that the inspectors are often unable to tell which processes have caused the defects they find, which makes it difficult to devise countermeasures. Even when the inspector does know the cause of a defect and reports it to the operator responsible, he or she is likely to get a response like "Oops, sorry!" and a vague promise to do better.

Level-two factories have thoroughly recognized the fundamental QC rule that quality is built into the product at each process. This means that the equipment operators who handle these processes should be responsible for inspecting their own products at the source.

This source inspection approach is often implemented incorrectly by managers who mistakenly think that it simply means assigning equipment operators the inspection tasks previously performed by inspectors. Without proper training, equipment operators will not be able to carry out effective inspections, and will instead pass along whatever "seems OK."

Corrective Action to Get to Level Three

Do not assign inspection work to equipment operators without providing adequate support and training.

The shift to source inspection by equipment operators must be managed carefully so that it doesn't become "no inspection." Supervisors and other managers are responsible for teaching operators how to distinguish defective goods from nondefective goods. To ensure an effective transition of inspection work to equipment operators, managers should:

- Write down inspection-related knowledge and techniques as work standards to help prevent defects.
- Give examples when the inspection criteria are subjective.
- Use pass/fail gauges to make dimensional inspections simple and reliable.
- Regularly inspect jigs, tools, and gauges used for inspecting products.

Important Point

- Help operators learn to distinguish accurately between defective and nondefective products.

Level Three

Inspection information is passed along immediately.

Defect prevention measures are taken promptly.

The defect rate has been reduced by at least half.

You cannot expect effective results from defect prevention measures that are based on statistics from final inspections. Even if such statistics are kept, they don't get back to the operator quickly enough to plan preventive measures.

At level two, plants have already implemented countermeasures such as recording inspection-related knowledge and techniques as work standards, using examples to aid subjective inspections, and regularly checking the jigs, tools, and gauges used for inspecting products. At level-three, factories have established a system for promptly relaying defect-related information so that simple and effective preventive action can be taken without delay. For example, a simple countermeasure for faulty subjective inspections is to have operators study examples and work within their parameters.

Corrective Action to Get to Level Four

Plan countermeasures that will completely eliminate defects.

Thoroughly implement source control.

Having sped up and improved the feedback and countermeasure process for defects at level three, to reach level four the factory must carry these efforts further by applying countermeasures at the source to completely prevent defects from recurring.

Measures are also needed to prevent defect production even when the operator is not paying attention to the equipment. For this, the factory must first achieve the "zero monitoring" goal (Key 7). The move to level four is supported by progress in other keys, such as quick changeover (Key 5), which ensures that even the first product made after changeover is free of defects.

Important Point

- Practice the "five whys" approach as part of source control.

Level Four

A mistake-proofing system is being built.

"To err is human," as the saying goes. This means you cannot depend on human attentiveness to eliminate defects. It also means that you must think of ways to prevent defect production even when the operator makes a mistake.

Such methods include *poka-yoke* (mistake-proofing) devices such as positioning pins to prevent setup errors (control-type poka-yoke) and sensors that automatically signal and stop the machine when a defect is made (warning-type poka-yoke).

In addition, the factory should establish a two-point inspection system whereby the operator at the next process double-checks products from the previous process and immediately notifies the previous process when a defect is discovered. Such two-point systems help operators prevent mistake-related defects and can dramatically reduce the defect rate overall.

Corrective Action to Get to Level Five

Track the abnormality rate (deviation from normal processing) rather than the defect rate.

The defect rate is usually calculated by dividing the total number of completed product units by the total number of manufactured units. This simple calculation method includes reworked units in the completed product total.

However, it is clear that items requiring even a little rework at a later process incur more defect-related costs than do defect-free items. Managers can account for such costs by using the abnormality rate as their management tool rather than the defect rate.

Using the abnormality rate also has other advantages. For example, at one plant that had reached level four by dramatically reducing its defect rate to just 0.1 percent, the new goal of cutting the defect rate in half (0.05 percent) didn't seem important enough to generate employee enthusiasm. However, when managers calculated the factory's abnormality rate and found it was well over 10 percent, improvement teams were anxious to cut it down and immediately started devising countermeasures.

Level Five

The entire factory has installed poka-yoke devices as part of their efforts to eliminate defects.

The abnormality rate is down to 0.1% or less and customer complaints are down to zero.

While the defect rate is typically calculated by taking off one point for each scrapped unit, the abnormality rate is calculated by taking off a point not only for each scrapped unit but also for each instance of reworking. This means that five points are subtracted if the same product unit is reworked five times during its manufacture.

The abnormality rate will thus exceed 100 percent if the average unit is reworked more than once. Clearly, reducing the amount of rework also reduces labor-hours and raises productivity. It follows that reducing the abnormality rate to a mere 0.1 percent will push labor costs down and productivity up and will help eliminate quality complaints from customers. Zero customer complaints is a sign of customer satisfaction, which always bodes well for product sales.

Level-five factories have taken the trouble to devise and install poka-yoke devices in most of their production equipment so that mistakes that have not been prevented are nevertheless automatically detected.

Key 12

Developing Your Suppliers

Cooperation and support for upstream processes and outside suppliers.

It is usually impossible for a manufacturing company to handle a product's entire manufacturing process from raw materials to finished goods. To establish the most efficient manufacturing configuration, it must find a balance between internal production and contracted external production. There is a saying in Japan that the supplier is a reflection of the purchaser—looking at a supplier will reveal much about the company being supplied. Cooperation between a manufacturer and its suppliers has an important impact on the manufacturer's quality, cost, and delivery.

Factories need to abandon the idea that their supplier relationships are simply sales transactions and recognize the wisdom of providing technical assistance to help suppliers improve their technology and manufacturing quality.

Training in value analysis (VA) and value engineering (VE) is one way manufacturers can help suppliers improve their processes and products. Sharing cost-cutting expertise with the supplier is another good area for cooperation. The effects are beneficial to both companies: the supplier becomes more competitive and the manufacturer is able to purchase higher-quality goods at lower cost and with more reliable delivery.

If manufacturers and their suppliers both take on the challenge of implementing the 20 Keys, both will gain new manufacturing strength and closer cooperation—two major ingredients for raising competitiveness.

This also applies to factory departments that do not use outside suppliers: downstream processes must lend support to upstream processes to ensure the quality of products coming downstream.

Level One

The manufacturer/ supplier relationship is limited to purchasing, acceptance inspections, and price negotiations.

A manufacturer/supplier relationship that is limited to purchasing, acceptance inspections, and price negotiations is the worst possible relationship from the perspective of revolutionizing manufacturing quality. Any factory that has such a relationship with its suppliers is a level-one factory.

At level-one factories, it is not surprising to find acceptance inspectors loudly complaining, "These are all rejects! Take them back!" and supplier representatives asking for a chance to do better but not really knowing where to start. In many cases, the supplier has been given plans, drawings, or manufacturing specifications that are simply not adequate to ensure desired product quality. The supplier is left guessing how to fill in the gaps and faces disrupted production whenever the client rejects a delivery.

Meanwhile, the client manufacturer's price negotiator is walking a fine line in pressuring the supplier to further cut costs. After all, there is a limit to how far any factory can cut costs without going into the red or sacrificing manufacturing quality. Putting too much pressure on suppliers only further erodes the quality of supplied parts.

Corrective Action to Get to Level Two

Manufacturers and suppliers must view each other as extensions of the same manufacturing flow.

On the one hand, the client factory's manager is complaining that critical parts haven't arrived, so the line has to be stopped. On the other hand, the supplier, hurrying to deliver the late parts, is moaning that it's not their fault because the client is asking too much. Neither party is looking the problem in the eye. As long as this situation lasts, neither party can expect production to get any smoother or easier.

Even though the supplier is responsible for part of the process that produces the final product, the client factory does not provide the supplier the same level of support as it provides to in-house manufacturing departments. Little wonder that supplier deliveries are late or that supplier product quality varies.

Thus, the first step is for the client factory to provide full support to suppliers just as it would for in-house departments.

Important Point

- Treat the outside supplier as you would an internal department.

Level Two

Technical assistance is given in response to supplier queries and problems.

In-house departments that do not use outside suppliers provide support to upstream departments.

At level-two factories, the department in charge of communicating with outside suppliers has in-house specialists available to answer any technical questions raised by suppliers and otherwise provide technical support.

For example, when a supplier reports difficulty making a part the way it was ordered, the client factory has an expert on hand who can suggest modifications or otherwise provide technical help to solve the problem.

In contrast to the level-one factory, suppliers for a level-two factory know exactly which of the client's departments to contact when a technical problem arises.

If the client factory shows a sincere interest in the supplier's operations (beyond prices) then relations can be improved to stabilize quality and create mutually advantageous cost/price structures.

Level-two factories have also started having in-house departments provide support for upstream in-house departments.

Corrective Action to Get to Level Three

Form joint VA/VE study groups with the supplier and link the two companies' improvement suggestion systems.

One good way to foster improvement of the supplier's operations is to establish joint VA/VE study groups that include frontline workers, managers, and engineers from the supplier factory. Often, the supplier lacks an adequate grasp of the client company's final product and its functions, which means the supplier may be using unnecessary or inefficient manufacturing processes. Joint study groups can clarify product knowledge and analyze manufacturing operations to eliminate such waste.

Such study groups also provide an occasion for training suppliers in IE methods, the use of operations improvement sheets, and other useful techniques.

Naturally, the client factory can expect more VA proposals from suppliers who have received adequate training in how to draft them.

Important Points

- Teach suppliers how to use IE methods and operations improvement sheets.
- Establish a system for encouraging and receiving improvement proposals from suppliers.
- Make sure in-house upstream processes also receive support from their downstream customers.

Level Three

Send technical support staff to the supplier factory.

Provide support in QC and IE methods for each of the supplier's production lines.

In today's global markets, competition in quality, cost, and delivery is especially harsh. Factories that use outside suppliers cannot limit improvement efforts to in-house departments and still hope to compete in these essential outputs. To be market leaders, they need lower costs and improved manufacturing quality everywhere, including at their supplier factories.

When a manufacturer begins to send technical support staff to its suppliers to train employees in QC and IE methods, it needs to go beyond simply responding to supplier questions (sign of a level-two factory) and take the initiative in identifying, explaining, and helping resolve the supplier's problems. This is level-three technical support.

However, even this level of technical support may result in only scattered labor cost reductions at the supplier company. At this point the client factory should avoid asking for specific cost reductions, as this might lead the supplier to believe that the improvement efforts are being implemented only to help the client factory cut costs.

Corrective Action to Get to Level Four

Recognize that partial implementation yields piecemeal results.

Encourage suppliers to help build a joint system for fully implementing the 20 Keys.

Implementing QC and/or IE techniques on specific processes or components works well only during high-growth periods when production volume is growing steadily. During slow-growth periods, suppliers that operate on a cost-plus basis have nothing to gain by cutting costs on specific process or components. Therefore, technical assistance in cutting supplier costs must not be limited in this way.

Many manufacturers use several different supplier factories. Since the 20 Keys approach strengthens all aspects of manufacturing at once, much greater effects can be achieved when the suppliers join the client factory in establishing a comprehensive 20 Keys implementation program.

Such programs operate best when the suppliers form a "supplier group" through which they can work together toward common goals.

Important Point

- Remember: Suppliers are a mirror of the client factory.

Level Four

The client factory and supplier factories have begun working together to implement the 20 Keys.

Step 1: 20 Keys study groups have been established among the supplier group or at individual supplier plants. Each supplier factory has evaluated its current level of manufacturing quality under the 20 Keys scoring system.

Step 2: Suppliers have implemented Key 1 (cleaning and organizing) and their factories have a whole new look. They understand the difference between conventional improvement methods and the 20 Keys approach.

Step 3: The client factory provides supplier training in Key 5 (quick changeover) and helps establish one or two model changeover examples at each supplier factory. These models clearly demonstrate the time saved by quick changeover and help supplier employees think differently about changeover.

Step 4: As part of implementing Key 2 (Rationalizing the system/management of objectives), advisors from the client factory hold multilevel meetings with supplier managers to identify common goals and align vectors toward achieving them. They also discuss what they hope to gain by reaching 20 Keys goals.

Step 5: The various companies start working in close cooperation to achieve the goals defined during the multilevel meetings. Each company is encouraged to report when they achieve doubled productivity in any part of their operations.

Step 6: The client factory provides ongoing support for its suppliers' 20 Keys implementation efforts.

Corrective Action to Get to Level Five

Each company is unique and must progress in its own way. The client factory should provide support attuned to each supplier's circumstances, including clear and specific advice on how to reach the next level.

The 20 Keys program is a lot for some supplier factories to digest all at once; sometimes it overwhelms them and stops their progress. When that happens, the client factory needs to take the initiative in offering support drawn from its own experience. Such support should be attuned specifically to the supplier's areas of difficulty to help the supplier make some progress in those areas.

The best approach in providing assistance to suppliers is to direct efforts specifically toward getting the supplier to the next level in each key. It is good to hold 20 Keys conferences once or twice a year so the client factory and its supplier group can proudly share their achievements and renew their mutual commitment to further progress. It is essential for everyone to realize that they are traveling together on the long road toward excellence.

Important Point

- Show them how to do it, then observe how they do it.

Level Five

Suppliers have improved their overall score by 20 points or have reached a 70-point total.

Neighboring in-house processes are working closely and solidly together.

Before the client factory can become a level-five factory, it must improve its overall score by 30 points or achieve at least an 80-point total. In addition, there must be ongoing progress at both the client factory and its suppliers.

Meanwhile, each supplier factory has improved its 20 Keys score by at least 20 points and has otherwise improved its manufacturing quality by shortening production periods, eliminating defects, etc. This has made suppliers more competitive, which makes them eligible for work from other clients and eventually leads to increased earnings.

At level five, suppliers are able to respond flexibly to orders from their client factory and, in many cases, are able to offer lower prices thanks to their higher productivity and lower costs. The mutual benefits enjoyed by the client factory and its suppliers motivate them to maintain and improve their close cooperation.

In factory departments that do not use outside suppliers, the attitude that the next process is the customer and that the previous process should provide support has taken hold and is being practiced with good effects.

Key 13

Eliminating Waste (Treasure Map)

All operations that do not add value are waste. A "Treasure Map" approach can make it enjoyable to hunt for waste.

When I visit factories, I often meet managers and frontline workers who do not really understand what waste is. For instance, I find managers who think that workers are being diligent and productive just because they are sweating away at physically tiring activities. The simple fact is that only work that adds value to the product is productive work. No matter how difficult or tiring an activity, if it does not add value, it does not get paid for and it is waste. It is important to make this point clear at the outset, before pursuing waste-reducing improvements.

Using a "Treasure Map" is an excellent way to help everyone understand what waste is and learn how to identify its various forms. In this approach, employee teams identify operations that can be improved and set up a map-style chart indicating current conditions around the plant and improvement goals. The map makes waste-hunting fun and positive by labeling problem areas "gold," "silver," or "copper" mines—gold being the most serious waste and the biggest value to be saved. Hunting waste with a Treasure Map can be done in fun and friendly competition between departments. The result is also agreeable: an efficient production system where waste is made obvious to everyone.

As wasteful operations are reduced, more time is freed for actual, value-adding operations that boost productivity.

Level One

People in the workplace have little understanding of waste.

Many managers think that brisk, arduous activity is a sure sign of productivity. When I start talking to such managers about making improvements, they say things like, "We're all too busy working." They think that making improvements would overwork their employees and hurt morale, so things are best left alone. Naturally, when I look around inside factories managed by such people, I find mountains of waste.

The first step in dispelling ignorance of waste is to realize that eliminating waste does not require extra effort. To the contrary, whenever waste is reduced, productivity rises, the work actually becomes easier, and the company becomes more competitive (and therefore more viable as a long-term employer).

Thus, there is no reason to put off the challenge of eliminating waste. Any plant where workers struggle with heavy objects or search for tools is a level-one factory when it comes to eliminating waste.

Corrective Action to Get to Level Two

People understand that all operations which do not add value are waste.

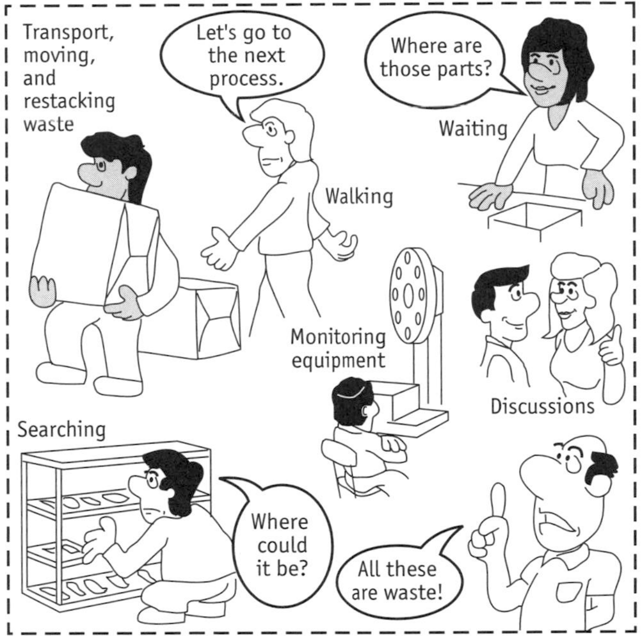

Recognizing that all operations which do not add value are waste, managers must carefully observe the various motions and actions workers use in their processes and identify clear instances of waste.

No matter how busy the workers seem as they carry inventory back and forth and load and unload pallets or shelves, these actions cannot be considered actual work since they do not add any value to the product. A customer will not be more interested in a product just because it was carried around the factory a lot. Customers pay for value, not for sweat.

What value is added to a product by the activity of searching for misplaced tools? How do idle time, discussions, and equipment monitoring directly add value to any product? How does the time and effort workers spend walking from one station to the next add value? Asking such questions will give a better picture of the benefits to be gained from eliminating wasteful activities.

Important Point

- Only do work that the customer will pay for—work that adds value to the product.

Level Two

Everyone shares a clear understanding of what waste really is.

Taking the new perspective that all activity that does not add value to the product is waste, everyone has resolved to make waste-reducing improvements.

The road ahead may be unclear at first. For example, an employee in the purchasing department may wonder, "If talking on the phone is waste, how can I do my job? I'm often on the phone." If you look at the various reasons for phone conversations, however, you will probably find that many calls are made to remind suppliers of delivery deadlines, to advise them of changes in the production schedule, and so on. Some of these calls could be avoided by faxing information or by having a more reliable production schedule. The idea is to reduce non-value-adding activities to the bare essentials by removing the causes for such activities.

Each factory employee should take a critical look at his or her own job activities and find where waste can be eliminated. Each waste-reducing improvement employees implement will help make products better, cheaper, and faster. Level-two factories are those where employees have all been taught in simple, everyday language what creates value and what makes waste.

Corrective Action to Get to Level Three

Make a Treasure Map for waste.

A Treasure Map provides an easy way to see where waste exists. Like gold, waste is a treasure because of the money you can make by digging it up. The Treasure Map categorizes waste into three levels of severity: activities that are extremely wasteful are mapped as mountainous "gold" mines while activities with progressively smaller degrees of wastefulness are mapped as "silver" and "copper" mines. Activities that appear to contain very little waste are labeled "flatlands." However, even the flatlands are worth digging into (for "oil"—hidden deposits of waste) after the treasure mines have been depleted.

The recommended approach is to divide the entire factory into workgroups that conduct work sampling studies. Based on their findings, a Treasure Map is made and displayed in a central location to show everyone where waste exists in various degrees. The groups then compete to eliminate the waste and raise the efficiency of their work.

Important Points

- Work sampling studies should have 95 percent reliability with a 3 percent margin of error.
- The job of work sampling should be shared by as many people as possible to lighten the load on the samplers and to ensure that everyone understands the need to identify and eliminate waste in their own department.
- The point of the Treasure Map is to make locations of waste (treasure) in the factory as visible as possible.

Level Three

The "treasure hunt" has begun.

Concrete results are being seen in some parts of the factory.

Based on factorywide work sampling studies, employees have created a Treasure Map showing locations of various degrees of waste. This has laid the groundwork for a friendly contest to raise the actual work ratio in each workplace. It should be emphasized that waste-eliminating improvements must be planned carefully to be effective. Level-three factories have begun making such improvements.

For example, it may be necessary to change the layout of a workplace to eliminate waste related to conveyance and/or walking. Implementing Key 1 (cleaning and organizing) helps eliminate searching waste, and Key 7 (zero monitor manufacturing) gets rid of equipment monitoring waste.

Study group sessions to share improvement results and learn how to raise the actual work ratio are good ways to focus improvement activities in the treasure hunt. The groups should look at where the actual work ratio is highest and where it is lower. Even though the treasure hunt is a kind of competition, cooperation is also important: any specific techniques for reducing waste and raising the actual work ratio should be shared so that everyone can draw from the factory's collective knowledge.

Corrective Action to Get to Level Four

Enthusiasm is not enough—concrete improvement plans are needed to dig out the mountains of treasure.

Measures to Raise Actual Work Ratio

	Previous round	Next measure	Current round	Next measure	Target
Actual work	73.0		79.2		85.0
Monitoring	5.8		4.1		3.0
Searching	2.4		2.2		1.7
Transport					

Before the study groups meet together to share results, each study group should draft some concrete waste-reducing improvement plans. The plans should include the work sampling data on current actual work ratios, along with descriptions of specific measures to be taken to increase those ratios and the target ratios aimed for. After presenting its results to the other study groups, the group that will be making the planned improvements should seek advice from managers and people from the other groups. This will help them fine-tune their improvement plans and can provide some new ideas for future improvements.

Work sampling studies should also take time factors into account. For example, such studies may determine that the actual work ratio dips on Mondays or near the start and end of each work day, or around the beginning of each month. Such data can provide clues as to which improvements will be most effective in raising the overall work ratio.

Important Point

- Study the gold, silver, and copper areas carefully and devise appropriate improvement measures.

Level Four

The overall actual work ratio has reached 85 percent or higher.

While enjoying the competition to dig up waste from the gold, silver, and copper treasure mines, the various study groups have raised the actual work ratio to at least 85 percent. This puts them at level four.

If you look at a factory that has achieved an actual work ratio of 85 percent or higher, you will see that everything—parts, tools, files, inventory, manuals, etc.—has been cleaned and organized, and a board clearly indicates today's and tomorrow's work operations. At each workplace, employees can look to their display board, labeled something like "Today's Job Assignments," to see what to do and when, eliminating the need for time-consuming discussions. At the end of the day, they can check the board for the next day's activities so they can get set up before they leave.

Equipment breakdowns have also been virtually eliminated—another reason why fewer discussions are needed—and there is little or no monitoring work. Production scheduling has also been well implemented so that there is now a smooth and clearly visible flow of materials through the factory, with little standby time for equipment operators. In offices, the implementation of one-page standards has eliminated the waste involved in stopping to think about work procedures.

Although some workplaces have more criteria to measure for their actual work ratio than others, progress in the above kinds of improvements will raise the actual work ratio to 85 percent and above. This is the synergistic result of making various specific improvements.

Corrective Action to Get to Level Five

Apply improvements in the other 19 keys toward further raising the actual work ratio.

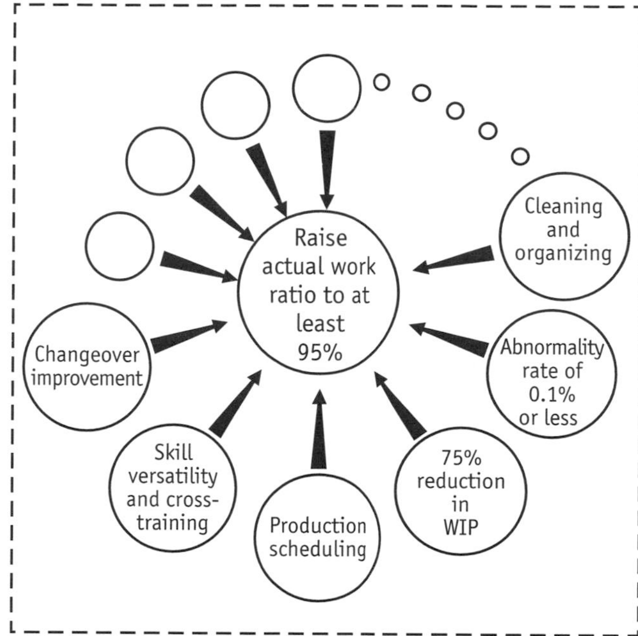

Once the factory has reached an actual work ratio of at least 85 percent, it is no longer so easy to find where waste is lurking. To raise the actual work ratio another 10 percent will require more than improvement measures that directly target the actual work ratio. It will require the synergy of improvements in the other 19 keys. Each technique that helps raise the other keys must be reexamined and appropriate improvement measures planned in a step-by-step program to gradually eliminate remaining non-value-adding operations.

For example, once a factory has reached level four or five in cleaning and organizing (Key 1), employees no longer have to make so many motions to get their work done. Layout improvements, a 75 percent reduction in work-in-process, the development of inventory stores between processes, and elimination of conveyance have also helped boost the actual work ratio. Skill versatility and cross-training have brought much more flexibility to job assignments and have helped to eliminate standby waste. The "single file" system in offices has made retrieval of information a quick and efficient process. People have learned to spend less time on the phone and to handle clerical procedures more smoothly, with less need for discussion.

Important Point

- Devise improvement plans to make everything in the factory easy to understand at a glance.

Level Five

The actual work ratio is at least 95 percent.

The factory has reached at least level four in the other 19 Keys.

In the level-five factory, employees are happy to realize that they are no longer wasting time and energy in making unnecessary motions and that they are being more productive while doing less physical work. There is no noticeable waste anywhere, and everyone's morale has been boosted by their collective efforts that created this wonderful new workplace. Everyone has a sense of pride and mutual gratitude in their achievement.

The level-five workplace cannot happen without across-the-board improvements, meaning progress to at least level four in the other 19 keys. The 20 Keys Matrix has helped everyone understand how these keys work synergistically to improve the basic QCD (quality, cost, and delivery) aspects of manufacturing strength.

The 20 Keys Matrix sets the 20 Keys as both row and column headings to produce a table of (20 x 20 =) 400 key combinations. (See pages 69, 111, 173, and 213 for examples of columns from the matrix.) It also helps to show how achieving a higher level in one key automatically brings multiple improvements across the board. This is how the 20 Keys approach makes the "impossible" possible.

Key 14

Empowering Workers to Make Improvements

Improvement Corners are created to showcase 20 Keys team accomplishments.

All 20 Keys require improvements that are easy to understand and therefore easy to maintain with no backsliding. Empowering workers to make improvements and setting up Improvement Corners are time-tested, concrete methods for doing just that.

Most improvements should be made during working hours, since their purpose is to make work go smoother and faster. It is also a basic principle that workplace improvements should be devised and implemented by the employees themselves; improvements made by others are less likely to meet employee needs. This means workers need to be empowered to devise and implement their own custom-made improvements. Improvement Corners are set up with tools and workspace for employees to use in implementing their ideas. When a team completes an improvement, it is displayed visually in the Improvement Corner, which highlights their success and helps other teams learn from their approach.

Future improvements are firmly rooted in past experience. This does not mean improvements should be done the same way in every circumstance—improvements must be fine-tuned for different situations. Like new product prototypes that go through a series of revisions and tests, workplace improvements don't always succeed on the first attempt—they too must be revised and reimplemented until successful results are obtained. Truly successful improvements are those which are well adapted to the workplace's circumstances—and only the workplace employees are capable of making such improvements.

Improvement Corner displays of new improvement ideas and how they work can easily become suggestions rewarded through the idea proposal system. They help raise morale and encourage others to implement similar improvements in their own workplaces.

Level One

Improvements are "someone else's job."

Level-one factories, even those that have an improvement suggestion system or a team-based approach for making improvements, still tend to have people outside the improvement-making team do the actual fabrication of newly designed equipment, tools, or jigs. Such dependence on outsiders makes the suggestion system less likely to produce bold new ideas and limits the scope of team activities.

Under such conditions, when an improvement team orders some new shelving to help clean and organize their workplace, the shelves that arrive may not be anything like what they really need. In some cases ordered supplies are so useless they have to be returned or discarded.

Some great improvement ideas from employees are thwarted by a lack of funds for implementation. Since it is impossible to predict where and how improvements will be needed, factory managers find it difficult to budget the required funds.

It is also a serious blow to morale when workers who have taken the trouble to devise a good improvement plan must wait until others can find the time and money to provide equipment needed for the improvement.

Corrective Action to Get to Level Two

Adopt a do-it-yourself policy for improvements.

Construct the first Improvement Corner.

Making improvements means applying experience and vision toward making things better. When improvement efforts go beyond planning to implementation, the results may or may not be what was envisioned in the improvement plan. Consequently, improvements must often be reviewed, revised, and reimplemented. This trial-and-error process becomes much more expensive when improvement teams must rely on others for the implementation work. Involving outsiders is also generally more troublesome and inconvenient than having a do-it-yourself improvement team.

If possible, construct the first Improvement Corner during working hours. Like operation improvements, the displays should be devised, built, and improved on by the improvement teams themselves so they serve each team's specific needs and approach. Having the improvement team members—mainly frontline workers—handle most of the implementation themselves adds an extra sense of pride to the displays.

Important Points

- Improvement Corners showcase team improvements and build pride.
- For greatest effect, improvements should be made during working hours.

Level Two

A model Improvement Corner has been completed.

Improvement teams are able to make their own shelves, tables, and platforms from sheet metal.

As progress is made in Key 1 (cleaning and organizing) and Key 4 (reducing inventory), a lot of factory floor space will be become available for other uses, including the construction of an Improvement Corner.

The Improvement Corner should include a sign announcing what it is and improvement exhibits that make it easy for viewers to see exactly how each improvement was made and what materials and tools were involved in implementing it.

A factory has reached level two when it has constructed at least one model Improvement Corner and has improvement teams that are able to make their own shelves, tables, and carts from sheet metal. Moreover, the members of these groups should have the materials and skills they need to work on improvements themselves when they get the chance during the work day. When improvement teams reach this level, their activities take on a new dimension of enthusiasm.

This approach also encourages workers to learn new skills they've always wanted to acquire, such as gas cutting and welding. This ties in with Key 15, skill versatility and cross-training. Improvement Corners also provide a convenient location for displaying safety information—a vital concern to help prevent accidents.

Corrective Action to Get to Level Three

Build an Improvement Corner near every major work area.

Expand the Improvement Corners' processing capabilities.

Generally, the idea is to have an Improvement Corner for each section or department in the factory. Particularly expensive items such as machine tools may have to be concentrated at certain Improvement Corners (those nearest to the machining department, welding department, etc.), but these corners should be made available to all workers for cross-training purposes.

Once several Improvement Corners are up and functioning, workers can visit them in spare moments during the day to get tips on how to tackle their own improvement projects. Seeing how other workers have built their own equipment and fixtures using welding and machining skills is sure to encourage Improvement Corner visitors to do likewise.

Naturally, empowering workers to do their own improvement-related welding and machining requires the establishment of a cross-training system to improve skill versatility.

Important Point

- Use space freed by cleaning and organizing and inventory reductions to set up Improvement Corners.

Level Three

Improvement Corners have been set up near every major work area.

Workers can make their own equipment and tools by machining, welding, etc.

Improvement teams are tackling the challenges of quick changeover.

Now that Improvement Corners have been set up near every major work area, it is easier for workers who have a few minutes free to apply the time toward making improvements. What they learn at these Improvement Corners helps them design and make drawings of equipment remodels and other workplace improvements that may even require the use of machine tools.

As progress in made in Key 5 (quick changeover technology), workers are now able to rebuild or modify their tools, jigs, and production equipment to facilitate quick changeover.

Nevertheless, there will always be items or processes such as finely honed precision parts, jig-boring, or tempering, that require equipment engineering expertise and skills, in which cases the work should be sent out to the appropriate in-house or external specialists. In such cases, it is very important to establish and maintain good communication between the equipment engineering specialists and the workers who are implementing the improvement.

Corrective Action to Get to Level Four

Provide in-house training in how to use equipment in the Improvement Corners.

Encourage workers to make mistake-proofing improvements using technology such as limit switches and photo sensors.

In addition to enhancing Improvement Corner displays and related training, the factory should have an education program through which workers can learn how to make improvements involving automation and labor-saving devices that are too complicated to display at Improvement Corners.

Educational displays of improvement equipment and technologies can be set up in exhibit rooms or other gathering places for factory employees to study. Such exhibits may include working examples of electromagnetic valves, limit switches, photoelectric sensors, and digital counters, along with instructions on pipe laying, wiring, and other aspects of installing and using such equipment. These exhibits will provide a convenient and useful way for workers to get guidance and ideas for their current improvement projects and concerns.

Important Point

- Set up an improvement equipment exhibit.

Level Four

The factory can build its own low-cost automation (LCA) devices and special-purpose machines.

It is ironic that many factories which manufacture robots do not have Improvement Corners and improvement equipment displays where workers can learn to build LCA devices or special-purpose machines.

In the level-four factory, workers are able to improve their productivity by custom-building their own LCA devices and special-purpose machines. If the desired equipment is too complicated for the workers to build themselves, the workers at least understand enough about the process of making it to explain to the equipment engineering specialists just what they need.

Workers often find ingenious uses for old discarded motors and parts in building unique LCAs and special-purpose machines.

Corrective Action to Get to Level Five

Offer training in the use of microprocessors and sensors.

To carry improvements even further, workers will need to learn about the latest relevant technologies. For example, microprocessors and sensors are essential ingredients when building LCA devices that are change adaptive.

Microprocessors and sensor devices are becoming increasingly more advanced and less expensive. Training workers in these types of technologies not only empowers them to make improvements but helps keep the entire factory up-to-date and competitive. It also provides a big boost toward automating production processes.

Indeed, LCA devices that are designed and built by the frontline workers who will use them are generally more practical and cost-efficient than expensive commercially available automation devices built by engineers.

Important Point

- The company should adopt a proactive policy toward adopting new technologies.

Level Five

The factory has made its own automation devices, such as automated parts detectors/sorters

Sensors are used in various ways.

Workers have learned to use information from Improvement Corners to turn old, discarded equipment into powerful, easy-to-use equipment. At this point, they have also acquired the knowledge needed to determine what the optimum equipment would be. Unlike workers in ordinary plants who take a long time to become proficient at using new equipment (usually ordered by someone in engineering), frontline employees in a level-five plant know exactly what they need to purchase to do the job and are ready to use it to its fullest potential.

Once factory workers have learned enough about the technologies involved, they can use microprocessors to build simple robots. If more sophisticated equipment is needed, they are expert enough to know what they want and how to use it to the best advantage. For example, workers at level-five factories have built autosorters that enable full-lot inspections as a final step to sort out defective products.

No matter how well trained the workers are, they will need additional periodic training to stay abreast of the latest advances and remain competitive.

Key 15

Skill Versatility and Cross-Training

Cross-training can be easy and fun!

At all too many factories, the unexpected absence of even one employee can cause line stoppages and other serious problems. Changing demand for products and the organizational changes required by the 20 Keys approach require factories to be flexible. Flexibility in the face of environmental changes is not possible without skill versatility—and that means more than learning the skills of others in your work group. It means learning the skills of various different job classifications.

A skills training program is needed. Since employees cannot all take courses at the same time, they should take the course that most directly relates to their current work so they can practice their new skills on the job. Later, employees should be rotated to different assignments that use different skills. A cross-training board should be posted to track employee assignments and skill achievements.

In implementing cross-training, managers must be careful not to rush the process by rotating people to new job assignments before they are ready for them. Make sure employees have a good grasp of the needed skills before moving them into new positions. It is a good idea to have at least two workers in each workshop reach the world class level (indicated by the double circle symbol on the cross-training board) in the skills at that workshop before rotating them to other job assignments.

Managers should expect the cross-training process to involve some temporary drawbacks, such as lower efficiency and production volume and higher costs due to the natural learning curve. These short-term disadvantages are worth it in the long run, when everyone understands each other's jobs and the factory has gained the manufacturing strength and competitive excellence of being truly change-adaptive.

Level One

No one is interested in skill versatility.

Although every factory has its "experts" who have mastered specialized skills not shared by others, in level-one factories managers think this is the way it should be, and they are happy if there is at least one expert in each workplace.

There is an old Japanese folktale about a famous swordmaker who possessed the secret to making the world's finest swords. He protected the value of his swords by never teaching anyone his professional secrets. He once caught another swordmaker trying to steal his secrets, and according to the story, he lopped off the man's arms to prevent him from ever making any swords. One could safely say that this swordmaker was opposed to skill versatility.

In level-one factories you will find many experts who are just as vehemently (if not violently) opposed to sharing their skills. Such experts are likely to say, "I'm the latheworking expert around here. You stick to your speciality and I'll stick to mine."

Specialist knowledge is guarded with particular zeal by technical staff, who tend to feel their jobs would be threatened if they shared their knowledge with frontline workers.

Corrective Action to Get to Level Two

Understand the need for skill versatility.

It used to be that factories could set their manufacturing schedule at the beginning of the month and follow it all the way to month's end. Factories now have to accept frequent schedule changes as a fact of life in an era of low growth and diversified demand.

At factories that are not sufficiently change-adaptive, managers find themselves stuck in the situation illustrated above: when one person is absent, the line stops. The other operators, being unable to fill in, become idle and are therefore as useless as the absentee.

At such times, managers become acutely aware of the need for skill versatility; everyone in the factory needs to share this awareness.

Important Point

- Introduce skill versatility as a theme for improvement team projects.

Level Two

Cross-training should begin within existing job groups.

In the level-two factory, improvement teams and everyone else understand the need for skill versatility. Meetings have been held to schedule cross-training for skill improvement and some cross-training courses have already been started.

Improvement team leaders have enlisted their teams' cooperation in overcoming problems caused by a lack of skill versatility. Employees are catching on to the pleasure of learning new skills. Some voluntarily ask for certain types of cross-training and they are eager to share their new skills with others.

Level-two factory managers know that workers need time to practice their new skills and try to accommodate that need by providing special times for cross-training. Worker attitudes are changing from "Oh no, not something new to learn!" to "I can use this chance to learn how to operate that machine."

In offices and other indirect departments, workgroup members are teaching each other so that everyone will eventually be able to do the work of anyone else in the group.

Corrective Action to Get to Level Three

Help everyone understand how interesting it is to have many skills.

Job	Lathe	Miller	Drill	Router
Joe	◎	○→◎	△→○	X→○
Fred	X→△	△→○	X→○	◎
Kathy	X→○	△→○	◎	X→△
Pat	△→○	X→△	○→◎	△→○

When the cross-training program is just getting under way, it is important that everyone look at the acquisition of new skills as a positive, interesting thing rather than a chore. Creative teaching methods can be used to make the learning process like a game. A visual aid such as a cross-training progress board posted in a conspicuous place becomes like a board game. The object is to earn as many double circles (the symbol for "fully trained") as possible. If you prefer numerical scores to symbols, just convert double circles, circles, and triangles to three points, two points, and one point. You can set a deadline date for ending each round of this board game, and then award some fun prizes to the winners.

Even aside from the question of cross-training, the 20 Keys approach also emphasizes the need for workers to constantly improve and refine their skills at their present job assignment. Therefore, a parallel schedule of skills training should also be implemented for skills related to existing job assignments.

Important Points

- Display the cross-training progress board in a conspicuous place.
- Have employees devise their own scoring system and goals.
- Do not forget the need for stabilization and further refinement of skills in current job assignments.

Level Three

Complete cross-training is being implemented within work groups.

The average worker has doubled his or her skills score.

In every workplace, employees are able to perform everyone else's work adequately (if not expertly). Equipment operators are watching their skill scores climb steadily. Moreover, jobs are not reassigned until the present workgroup includes at least two "experts" who have fully mastered the work operations in that group (and therefore rate a score of three for the corresponding skills on the cross-training progress board). If the average worker has doubled his or her total skill score, the factory has reached level three.

Some workplaces may contain equipment (such as certain NC machines) that is complicated enough to require specialists to run it. However, even such equipment can be made more accessible to regular workers through 20 Keys improvements such as quick changeover, consistent use of quantified descriptions in instructions, and elimination of fine-tuning.

Rotating employee assignments to train people on all equipment in the workplace is only aspect of promoting cross-training. Another important way is to modify the equipment to make it more user-friendly. In assembly processes, the various operations can be learned more quickly through the use of custom-made jigs and clear explanations of standard operating procedures.

Corrective Action to Get to Level Four

The entire factory is actively learning new skills in various job classifications.

One-page standards simplify cross-training for administrative staff.

A comprehensive program is essential to implement cross-training plantwide so the factory can adapt to any imaginable change.

Some people say it takes about ten years for someone to fully master the operation of a particular lathe. Does that mean it will take several decades to cross-train operators in a variety of machines? Some machines do not require much training, such as NC machines where operators simply remove the processed workpiece, set up the next one, and then press a button. It is also possible to modify equipment to make it easier to operate, such as by fitting positioners onto welding equipment so that only downward welding is required.

In administrative departments, one-page standards make it easy for anyone to see how to do a particular task.

Important Points

- Modify machines so that operators from different job classifications can run them.
- Use one-page standards so that even inexperienced office workers can easily learn work procedures.

Level Four

Everyone has embraced the goal of creating an adaptable factory.

Cross-training across job classifications has begun.

The level-four factory has made enough progress in cross-training operators that the factory can respond more rapidly to production scheduling changes by reassigning operators as needed. As this cross-training program continues, the machinists, welders, and painter/coaters are teaching each other their respective skills. The employees have a positive attitude and enjoy acquiring new skills.

Meanwhile, several "master" operators are kept on hand in their respective job classifications to ensure an overall high level of skilled labor on the production line.

At level four, the factory is able to plan how to redistribute its labor resources to accommodate various types of production changes. They are carrying out a cross-training program to create the most effective mix of skills among the operators. A cross-training progress board is displayed in a conspicuous place where everyone can see it, including visitors.

Some factories can carry cross-training to the point where even office workers are trained and qualified to help out on the production line when necessary. In any case, everyone in the company now understands the need for cross-training to make the company more adaptive and competitive.

Important Point

- Operations throughout the entire factory should become adaptable to change.

Corrective Action to Get to Level Five

Reach level four or five in Key 1 (cleaning and organizing) to eliminate wasteful motion.

Implement Key 1 (cleaning and organizing) to the point where operators can work with everything they need laid out neatly, easily within reach, and easily visible via appropriate labeling. Work standards, product samples, measurement tools, and poka-yoke devices have been set up at each station to help prevent defects. Stores between stations enable operators to quickly get any materials they need, there is a clearly marked place for them to put their finished goods, and an operations board clearly indicates what to do now and what to do next.

At this level, the single-minute changeover achieved by implementing Key 5 (quick changeover technology) enables any operator to perform changeover quickly and flawlessly—even the first product after the changeover is defect-free. Moreover, the production equipment is well maintained so it can continue to operate in top, defect-free condition.

Implementation of this and the other 19 keys has created a factory where anyone can perform a variety of jobs without making mistakes.

Important Point

- Reach level four or five in the other 19 keys.

Level Five

The factory is fully able to adapt to change by reassigning trained employees.

Although not all operators are able to operate all types of equipment or perform all types of assembly work, enough have been cross-trained so that the plant's managers can reassign workers without difficulty in order to meet any kind of change in production scheduling.

With the progress made in other keys (especially Key 7, zero monitor manufacturing), almost all operators can now handle several pieces of equipment and many are learning to handle several machines in different job classifications as well.

The cross-training progress board at a level-five factory shows that many operators have acquired the "master" level (double circle or three points) in new job skills, which has helped raise the overall skill level of the factory's work force. In offices and other staff departments, complete implementation of one-page standards has torn down the walls between job classifications and enabled people to ably assist their colleagues in other sections or departments when necessary.

Key 16

Production Scheduling

Production scheduling: a key support for bolstering manufacturing quality.

Every production manager dreams of always being able to meet delivery deadlines without idle or standby time for workers or equipment. Today's uncertainty in demand predictions, diversification of needs, challenging specifications, shorter lead times, and greater fluctuation of demand make this dream harder than ever to achieve. Yesterday's desktop production scheduling methods are totally inadequate for today's factory. Making production scheduling smooth requires progress in other interrelated keys to improve the company's overall manufacturing quality.

Production scheduling is a management method for ensuring that goods and/or information are provided to customers on time. The 20 Keys approach to production scheduling is rooted in the principle that the next process is the customer; therefore each process should be responsible for delivering on time to the next process. Each process is also evaluated and scored on how much it contributes toward on-schedule delivery. This principle applies to administrative and staff processes as well.

The idea of "customers" appears at various points in the 20 Keys. You could think in terms of "users" rather than "customers," since most of these customers are intermediate processes far removed from the actual end users who pay for the products. Nevertheless, each process should be evaluated as to how well it serves the next process and whether its employees work to satisfy the needs of the next process's staff as if they were end-user customers.

Level One

Deliveries are rarely on schedule.

Production scheduling at the level-one factory is a confused mess. Production managers are stuck between a rock and a hard place: on the one hand, customers are upset that deliveries are late and want their orders to get top priority. On the other hand, workers are not sure what to do since the managers keep expediting orders and changing priorities in response to customer requests.

This example may sound a bit extreme, but plenty of factories have production scheduling that is almost this bad. They try to use traditional ledger-based production scheduling for today's complicated manufacturing systems.

This traditional method emphasizes only order volume and delivery schedules and relies on the intuition and constant attention of production managers. Production managers try to adjust production to suit customer needs by inserting rush items into the line at various points and/or rearranging the sequence of processes, which causes mass confusion, frustrates the equipment operators, and lowers productivity.

Level Two

Start/completion boards are constructed.

Start/completion boards are made for each batch of order information, although the scheduling on these boards may be only approximate.

These boards indicate not only the completion dates for each part but also the dates for starting production of each part. Having the start/completion dates on a single board that is prominently displayed in the factory is the first step in the 20 Keys approach to production scheduling.

Of course, there is more to this approach than simply posting start/completion boards. Even after the production schedule has been sent to the factory, production managers should meet weekly if not daily to track production and arrange for any needed changes. Managers must also take measures to clearly inform the frontline workers about the production sequence and any changes that are made in it. In addition, they should establish checkpoints at various milestones between a product's start and completion dates to help track production.

Start/completion boards should also be used in administrative and staff departments to clearly indicate the approximate amounts of time required for various work operations.

Problems at Level Two

Some products are still late for delivery.

Production tends to get especially busy toward the end of each month.

Level-two factories still have trouble getting all orders delivered on time. Even though managers are controlling the production starts and tracking orders throughout production to make sure they stay on schedule, sometimes an order is still not delivered on time.

One reason for this problem is that the equipment and labor capacity at each process has not been clearly defined, so processes may end up overburdened, creating production bottlenecks that can result in late deliveries.

Level-two factories are also still prone to end-of-the-month rushes as upper managers pressure factory managers to turn out enough goods for the sales department, which is trying meet a sales target.

Whereas level-one factories get their customers angry enough to come to the factory to complain, the customers of level-two factories have less to complain about and often just call in their complaints.

Level Three

All products are written up on process flowcharts that track everything from preparation of raw materials to final assembly.

A tracking form is attached to all work orders.

Production scheduling should include everything from preparation of raw materials to completion of the final product. Process flowcharts for each product should be standardized and posted for reference, based on a careful consideration of all the production steps for each product. Managers also need to consider the labor and equipment capacities of each process to prevent bottlenecks and achieve leveled production. In addition to monthly schedules, weekly and daily schedules should also be worked out and posted in the factory. The shorter-range schedules will let factory workers know exactly what they will be doing today and tomorrow, so they recognize quickly if they are behind schedule. For example, the schedules should indicate the standard (average) amount of time materials and/or inventory should remain at each station for processing. That way standard processing schedules can be calculated and followed and everyone can see which parts should reach which process by which time.

Other types of schedules, such as 20 Keys action plans, can be used in offices and staff departments to help managers and workers track work-in-process.

Important Points

- Level the work operations throughout the month to avoid end-of-month rushes.
- Spread out workloads to prevent bottlenecks.

Problems at Level Three

Discuss occasional product delays with the customer to minimize the inconvenience.

Once corrective action has been taken to reach level three, most products will not be late for delivery and production managers will have enough control of production to explain any delays and assure customers as to when late products will be completed. They will also be better able to adjust the production schedule to accommodate rush orders when necessary without creating a chaotic production situation.

At this level, production managers are aware that the production system needs more flexibility in parts supplies and labor capacity to accommodate schedule adjustments.

One might wonder why a factory with level-three production scheduling would still be plagued by late deliveries. The reason is that such factories have only reached level three in the other 19 keys as well. This means that there are still some equipment breakdowns, quality defects, incomplete 4S implementation, lack of skill versatility, inadequate time control policies, weak connections between processes, and other problems that weaken the overall manufacturing quality and therefore prevent delay-free production. Production managers should recognize such shortcomings as the root causes of many types of production problems.

Level Four

The plant manages to make all deliveries on time.

Delays in shipments to customers have finally been eliminated, thanks in part to the new customer-focused attitude that keeps goods moving on schedule from process to process. No longer do production managers have to meet with unhappy customers about late deliveries.

The foundations for this success were already laid at level three, but it took progress beyond level three in the other 19 keys to enable the total elimination of production delays. For example, now that the factory has reached at least level three in Key 17 (efficiency control), standard labor-hours can be reliably estimated for each process and used as a process capacity reference when drafting production schedules and issuing work orders. To help processes maintain their expected operating efficiency, help them track their status by displaying various yield figures that are pegged to efficiency levels.

Likewise, a factory with level-four production scheduling must have reached at least level three in other keys relating to quick changeover, process coupling, elimination of the causes of equipment breakdowns, cross-training for skill versatility within work groups, and computer-based production scheduling.

Important Point

- Reach level three or higher in the other 19 keys.

Problems at Level Four

Work is still coming in waves.

On the surface, the level-four factory appears to have a very smooth-running production system, but if you check closely you will find that some work groups are working overtime now and then to stay on schedule. At the same time, some work groups occasionally encounter slow periods; they have finished their current job and have not yet reached the start time for the next job. In other words, work is coming in waves, and the production manager's job is to somehow even out the work flow and avoid the waves.

This problem is partly due to incomplete (level three or four) implementation of the other 19 keys. For instance, the factory has managed to drastically reduce equipment breakdowns but has not yet totally eliminated them; the labor force has not received enough cross-training to make the factory fully adaptive to changes; and defects still occur now and then. Because these keys are all interrelated, having room for improvement in some keys means there is still some room for improvement in the other keys too.

Level Five

All deliveries are made on time, with no stress.

Now the factory is able to produce the right amount of the right product at the right time and without undue stress or confusion. Production managers can guarantee satisfactory delivery timing, production capacity, and product quality even for high-priority orders, and without overworking employees.

Level Five

(continued)

On-time delivery, sufficient production capacity, and satisfactory quality are assured even for rush orders.

Production smoothing and cross-training have eliminated production fluctuations.

All of the 20 keys are intimately related to assurance of timely delivery, and a factory that ignores any one of these keys will be unable to reach level five in production scheduling. Improvement in production scheduling skills by itself is not enough to ensure on-time delivery, but comprehensive 20 Keys improvement will add so much strength to the company's manufacturing quality that what used to seem impossible will now seem easy to the factory that has reached level four in all 20 Keys.

20 Keys Matrix

Target Key: Key 16–Production Scheduling

Countermeasures for related keys to help improve the target key.	
1. Cleaning and organizing	Mark areas with dividing lines and get rid of unneeded stuff to make the flow of goods easy to see.
2. Rationalizing the system/ management of objectives	Make sure everyone understands the importance of meeting deadlines.
3. Improvement teams	Have teams within and between work groups cooperate in meeting deadlines.
4. Reducing inventory	Level production so that only what is needed is being manufactured.
5. Quick changeover	Achieve single changeover to facilitate small-lot production.
6. Manufacturing value analysis	Implement operation improvements to shorten production and accommodate rush orders.
7. Zero monitor manufacturing	Use "one-page standards" to achieve a waste-free flow of clerical operations.
8. Coupled manufacturing	Smooth the flow of factory work to make the management board more reliable.
9. Maintaining equipment	Root out and eliminate causes of breakdowns and line stoppages to make the management board more reliable.
10. Time control and commitment	Eliminate wasted time, early clock-out, etc.
11. Quality assurance system	Eliminate rejects due to quality defects to make production scheduling more reliable.
12. Developing your suppliers	Provide guidance and in-house models for suppliers concerning the use of management boards, etc.
13. Eliminating waste ("treasure map")	Eliminate wasteful work motions and transportation to help keep production on schedule.
14. Empowering workers	Encourage modifying improvements and better use of management boards.
15. Skill versatility and cross-training	Train everyone to learn equal skill levels in various jobs to achieve flexibility that helps meet deadlines.
16. Production scheduling	
17. Efficiency control	Use graphs to track efficiency improvement and motivate further efficiency improvements.
18. Using information systems	Use microprocessors in POP devices and other devices to speed up production management.
19. Conserving energy and materials	Implement energy- and resource-saving improvements to streamline manufacturing and help meet deadlines.
20. Leading technology/ site technology	Introduce new technologies, such as computer-based technologies, to improve production scheduling abilities.

Key 17

Efficiency Control

Efficiency control can be a motivation booster.

No matter how many interesting ideas are presented for improving factory productivity, factory employees are not likely to get behind any idea that does not support and recognize their own contributions. Factories need to develop efficiency control systems that are understood and supported by frontline workers as well as managers.

One way to do this is by making simple graphs that show goals as numerical values and graphically display efficiency changes so everyone can clearly see the effects of their improvement efforts. The multifaceted 20 Keys approach encourages everyone to contribute their strength and ingenuity to reach these goals. Within the context of the 20 Keys, even the pursuit of efficiency control can be a motivational activity.

High-motivation efficiency control must be carried out with careful consideration to supporting and rewarding each employee's efforts. The 20 Keys approach does this by presenting common goals for managers and frontline workers and by having everyone work together toward achieving them. This approach improves efficiency control for the sake of the entire company.

Frontline employees will not feel inclined to work toward greater efficiency and higher productivity if their work is not properly evaluated. They need to know when they are improving or backsliding and they need to see that their supervisors are seriously concerned about making improvements. The same is true in offices and other staff departments.

It is also important to train employees so they are better able to devise improvements and lay the groundwork for enhancing efficiency control. The companywide 20 Keys approach builds the manufacturing quality and strength needed to reach efficiency control goals in a way that motivates everyone.

Level One

Indirect "efficiency control" reporting is used.

A factory manager cannot even speak of having an efficiency control system if there are no factorywide and station-specific goals or if these goals are not clear to everyone.

Many factories rely on indirect efficiency control reporting, such as the amount of profit per employee, which ties efficiency to the sales prices of products. Such factories are clearly level-one factories when it comes to efficiency control.

To take a concrete example, suppose that a certain factory sets its efficiency goals based on how many tons of foundry castings per employee are sold per month (the month's total sales divided by the number of factory employees). Naturally, a higher profit-per-employee figure means better business results for management. Nevertheless, it's not helpful to tell the factory workers to "produce 10 tons of castings per employee this month to gross $1.5 million in sales vs. $800,000 in manufacturing costs." Most workers will not be able to relate to such figures. However, they do sense that efficiency goals are much easier to reach for some products than for others. Moreover, they realize that success or failure in sales has more to do with sales efforts and quantities ordered than with the efforts of individual factory workers.

Managers also need to have meaningful efficiency evaluation methods, so they can provide real support for employees instead of just saying, "See what you can do to increase your efficiency."

Corrective Action to Get to Level Two

Avoid counting process steps in wide-variety small-lot production by defining product groups and estimating the number of steps per group.

Returning to the foundry example, managers there might determine the relative ease or difficulty of a foundry job according to the number of cores in the castings. Or they might use their experience-based intuition to select several conversion indices from the casting drawings. Then they work with the experienced operators to group the jobs according to difficulty, labeling them A, B, or C. Use additional groupings if the products appear to belong to an entirely different level of difficulty. If the product has much in common with previous products, the managers can apply the data from those products to determine the difficulty level. This method can also be used to indicate the amount of work needed to manufacture the product in question.

One could also obtain a general indication of efficiency by determining standard times for each difficulty level (such as "Level A jobs require X number of minutes to make one ton of product") and then comparing these standard time figures to the total actual time.

A general method that operators can relate to is better than a more precise method that they find irrelevant, because the former can help raise operators' concerns about efficiency and spark their interest in making improvements.

Level Two

Products are divided into families.

Standard labor content is calculated for each product family.

Production levels in each family are used to determine the factory's labor efficiency.

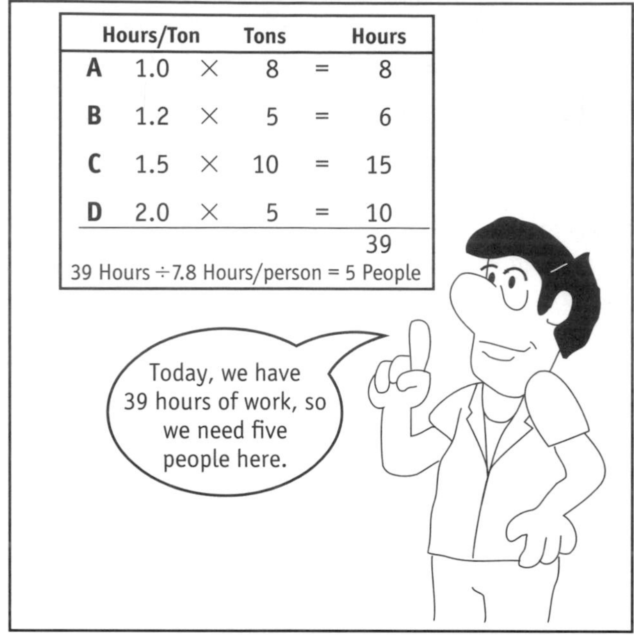

	Hours/Ton		Tons		Hours
A	1.0	×	8	=	8
B	1.2	×	5	=	6
C	1.5	×	10	=	15
D	2.0	×	5	=	10
					39

39 Hours ÷ 7.8 Hours/person = 5 People

Managers use standard labor content per product family to determine the total number of labor-hours required, as shown in the illustration. This requires the establishment of the following seven preconditions:

1. A daily work schedule has been written for each operator.
2. Standard work times have been determined for each product model.
3. Basic families (difficulty levels) of products have been determined.
4. Operators feel that their supervisors and colleagues understand and appreciate the effort they put into their work.
5. Managers have set up and maintain monthly efficiency charts for each work group.
6. All efficiency control is based on numerical data.
7. Difficulty indices and standard times are reviewed periodically.

Corrective Action to Get to Level Three

Determine standard times for each process and set up a method for obtaining actual times to use for efficiency control.

Before attempting efficiency control, determine a standard time for each process. The method used to calculate the value of labor sometimes can be used to calculate the labor time for each process as well.

Standard processing time is the amount of time it takes an experienced employee (i.e., one with all the required skills) to operate the process with an appropriate level of effort under normal working conditions. Some companies estimate labor times with methods like work-factor (WF), methods time measurement (MTM), or the modular arrangement of predetermined times system (MODAPTS), or predetermined motion time study (PTS). Other companies just use a stopwatch to measure actual processing time, then calculate standard times based on the timed samples of actual work.

However, an even simpler alternative is to use the previous year's actual work time statistics as the basis for determining standard times to control the efficiency of this year's work. This method yields a more change-adaptive type of efficiency control that is more relevant to frontline workers and therefore more likely to attract their interest.

Important Point

- Decide which time value calculation method is most appropriate for your factory.

Level Three

Standard times have been determined for each process, actual times have been obtained, and efficiency control has begun for various processes.

Labor content has been calculated.

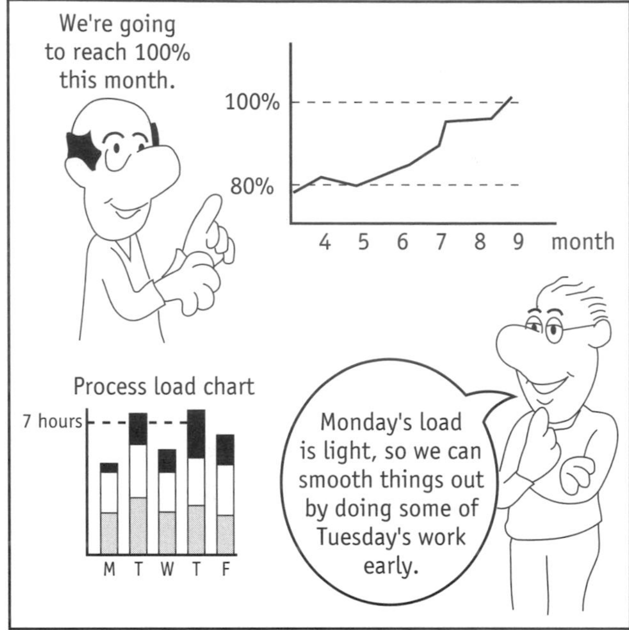

Factory managers have begun implementing efficiency control for various processes and have calculated the processes' labor content based on a standard unit of labor (such as standard times). The plant is at level three when the following conditions are met:

1. Standard times are set for all major product models and operations.
2. Actual times have been obtained for all product models and operations.
3. Efficiency control is implemented for all primary operations.
4. Efficiency control graphs display monthly targets for each work group.
5. Standard labor hours are used to determine labor content for each process and jobs are assigned accordingly.
6. Efficiency control graphs are in place to display daily targets for each work group.
7. Standard times are periodically reviewed and revised.

The labor content calculations should be smooth and reliable so they can be used to plan average loads on a daily, weekly, and monthly basis.

Important Point

- Periodically review and revise standard times.

Corrective Action to Get to Level Four

Carry out efficiency control for all operations.

Set standard times for all operations. Standard times are easier to set for some operations than for others. Use past experience as a basis for estimating standard times for special-order products and prototypes so that they can be included with all other operations as targets of efficiency control.

Next, implement operating rate control. The operating rate is calculated by dividing the total working hours by the actual operation time and then multiplying by 100. In this case, the actual operation time is found by subtracting nonworking time from total working hours.

To calculate the required number of workers, divide the total standard time by the product of the estimated efficiency and the estimated operating rate. If the efficiency and operating rate are properly controlled, the calculations of the required number of workers should be accurate.

Efficiency control graphs should be posted in conspicuous places, where operators and supervisors can enter data every day to track their efficiency ratings. This will enable them to see right away when efficiency has dropped so they can take prompt corrective action.

Level Four

Efficiency control is being carried out for individuals or work groups in all operations.

Employees throughout level-four factories are fired up and ready to achieve their efficiency goals. As progress in made in efficiency control, managers are able to track how much individuals or work groups are contributing to efficiency. Managers can clearly see people's enthusiasm for improving efficiency.

The level-four factory has established the following conditions for efficiency control:

1. Efficiency control is being used for prototypes and special-order products as well.
2. Daily efficiency is tracked for individuals or work groups in all operations.
3. Daily efficiency control graphs are displayed and used to detect day-to-day drops in efficiency, which are promptly addressed with corrective action.
4. Operating rate control is also being carried out.
5. Efficiency and operating rate estimates are used to plan labor requirements for the next month.
6. The factory has reached level three or higher in the other 19 keys.
   Everyone is confident about reaching their efficiency goals and enthusiastic about tracking their progress.

Important Point

- Achieve level three or higher in the other 19 keys.

Corrective Action to Get to Level Five

First reach at least level four in the other 19 keys.

Keep efficiency control accurate and useful.

Despite the frequent changes in customer needs and product models and the ongoing development of new products, new technologies, and new manufacturing methods, some factories insist on maintaining the same standard times for their operations.

Consequently, standard times at these plants become less accurate and believable, and workers become disenchanted with the efficiency control system. Standard times must be reviewed and revised regularly so that they can remain useful for accurate efficiency control.

Make sure efficiency goals are appropriate for the circumstances. If efficiency goals are too difficult to reach, workers will become discouraged and will lose their enthusiasm for improvement.

To reach level five, the factory must be able to set and meet appropriate efficiency goals and must have attained at least level four in the other 19 Keys.

Important Point

- Keep efficiency control current and accurate enough to complement production scheduling.

Level Five

Efficiency control is accurate and relevant enough to sustain everyone's enthusiasm.

Everyone is confident about reaching suitably challenging efficiency goals.

Workers in the level-five factory consistently meet their efficiency goals. Work loads for various operations and equipment are easily balanced by managing the standard time and cycle time data. Production scheduling is carried out at the level of individual machines and production leveling is carried out based on average labor times.

The level-five factory has established the following conditions for efficiency control:

1. Everyone is motivated to reach their efficiency goals.
2. Everyone is confident about reaching their efficiency goals.
3. Workers feel their efforts are rewarded as they check and update their efficiency control graphs.
4. Everyone understands how efficiency control depends on progress in the other 19 keys.
5. Everyone takes interest in the efficiency trends shown on the efficiency control graphs.
6. Workers consistently meet their efficiency goals, which makes it easier to meet the production schedules.

Key 18

Using Information Systems

Microprocessors: an essential ingredient for better manufacturing quality.

Microprocessors were originally developed as large-scale integrated circuits (LSIs) for powerful mainframe computers. Today, advanced integration levels and cost reductions have brought them into offices in equipment such as personal computers, photocopiers, and fax machines. In factories, they are applied in labor-saving numerically controlled (NC) machines and in advanced automation equipment such as industrial robots, welders, and painter/coaters. The range of microprocessor applications continues to widen as new sensor and image processing technologies are applied in production equipment.

Today, most manufacturing companies are already using these types of equipment in office automation (OA) and factory automation (FA) applications. More ambitious companies are developing comprehensive OA/FA systems that use point of production (POP) information management, computer-integrated manufacturing (CIM), and strategic information system (SIS) technologies to coordinate and integrate information processing and management throughout the factory, company, or regional group of companies.

Remember, however, that computers are just computers. To make any manufacturing system work, you need not only good computers but good employees who can adapt promptly to changes.

This human factor tends to be the biggest bottleneck when developing a CIM system or something similar. The 20 Keys approach coordinates the development of computer software applications with the current level of achievement in improving manufacturing quality so that new software applications can be put to effective use immediately without confusion or failures.

Level One

No one even thinks of using even simple technologically controlled equipment

The level-one factory is too complacent to take much notice of modern technology and its applications. Veteran equipment operators may even feel defensive about such technologies, and argue "It's better to have a skilled operator do that," or "There's nothing wrong with the way we've being doing it."

Despite the prejudice often expressed by operators, supervisors, and even managers, computer technology is used in so many ways today that even those who disdain it are enjoying its benefits.

Modern technology and its applications have many names, from LSIs to VLSIs (very large scale integrated circuits) and ultra-VLSIs to computer systems such as personal computers and workstations, and so on. For simplicity's sake, the 20 Keys approach uses the term "information technology" broadly to include all of these applications.

Corrective Action to Get to Level Two

Recognize that using more numerical data for goals creates a greater need for microprocessor applications.

When 20 Keys action plan charts are used to track progress in the various keys, the manual entry of so much numerical data means that there are likely to be errors in transcribing, which is a rather slow and inefficient process anyway. Factories need to recognize the potential gains in accuracy and efficiency that can come from using computers to enter and manage numerical data in action plans, production schedules, and other areas. Use of information technology is essential for advancing to top levels in the 20 Keys.

Production managers should also recognize how NC machines and other factory automation equipment can aid their development of multiprocess handling by multiskilled operators.

The first step is for managers and operators to get a general grasp of what OA and FA equipment is, how it is used, and what benefits can be expected, so that they can relate this equipment to their own work.

Important Point

- Set up or visit OA/FA exhibits to learn about these technologies.

Level Two

OA and FA applications are used in limited areas.

Using commercially available systems, the level-two factory has introduced OA or FA applications in limited areas such as production scheduling, staff management, quality control, and making estimates. Moreover, managers are interested in OA and FA not only because these technologies are in fashion, but also because they recognize the benefits to be gained, such as preventing data transcription errors.

With the introduction of NC machines, some machinists are now able to handle several processes at once. Some electronically controlled machining centers can operate unassisted throughout the day and night, thereby raising the equipment operating rate. Other sophisticated FA equipment, such as welding robots, 3-D measuring instruments, and NC punch presses are being introduced to help achieve improvement goals in productivity and quality, and frontline operators are busy learning how to use these new machines.

Corrective Action to Get to Level Three

Expand progress in the 20 Keys, including staff departments.

Once the factory has begun introducing microprocessor-based applications in its offices and other indirect departments and has reached level two or three in the other 19 keys, it is ready to smoothly develop factory- or companywide integrated OA/FA/POP systems.

Also, as the factory gets closer to level three in all 20 keys, supervisors and managers are better able to identify needs for integrated automation systems. They can then introduce and adapt these systems to meet specific needs, which makes such systems even more cost-effective.

Progress in the other 19 keys is a prerequisite for introducing integrated OA/FA/POP systems. The factory's manufacturing quality must reach a sufficiently advanced level through the 20 Keys program that its components (departments or work groups) are cohesive and efficient enough to adopt one of these systems without spending many months learning to use it well.

Important Point

- Get to level two or three in the other 19 keys.

Level Three

A factory- or company-wide OA/FA integrated system has been developed.

A POP system is in use.

The level-three factory has networked its computers and set up systems for sharing software programs and data among the various departments. This integration of previously separate systems has brought the factory to a new level of efficiency.

On the factory floor, a POP system is up and running, enabling production data to be gathered directly by wire or indirectly (such as via a bar code reader) from the production stations. The factory is able to function flexibly as a wide-variety, small-lot production system that takes advantage of automation technologies in machine tools, autowarehousing, autoconveyance, assembly and welding robots, etc. These various machines and systems are integrated within the same flexible manufacturing system (FMS) for maximum efficiency.

The factory has also introduced other advanced applications such as computer-aided design and computer-aided manufacturing (CAD/CAM) systems for product design and development, and communication links to various controllers as part of the factory's FMS.

Corrective Action to Get to Level Four

Implement the 20 Keys to level four in all departments.

As the company, including staff departments, approaches level four in the 20 Keys, the various separate strands of improvement are systematically brought together, enabling the formation of a truly effective computer integrated manufacturing (CIM) system. The nucleus of this CIM system is the database of company information that has been unified in format and processing flow so that it can be effectively used throughout the company.

This rationalization and integration of information and communication throughout the company helps everyone in the company feel they are playing on the same team and can respond to changes with smooth teamwork. (This is the "baseball-style" teamwork that characterizes level four in Key 2, rationalizing the system/management of objectives.) As much as possible, everyone should strive to use similar methods in pursuing similar goals.

Important Point

- Get to level three or four in the other 19 keys.

Level Four

The CIM system has been fine-tuned for the company's needs.

The POP system is fully implemented and factories and offices have implemented paperless record-keeping.

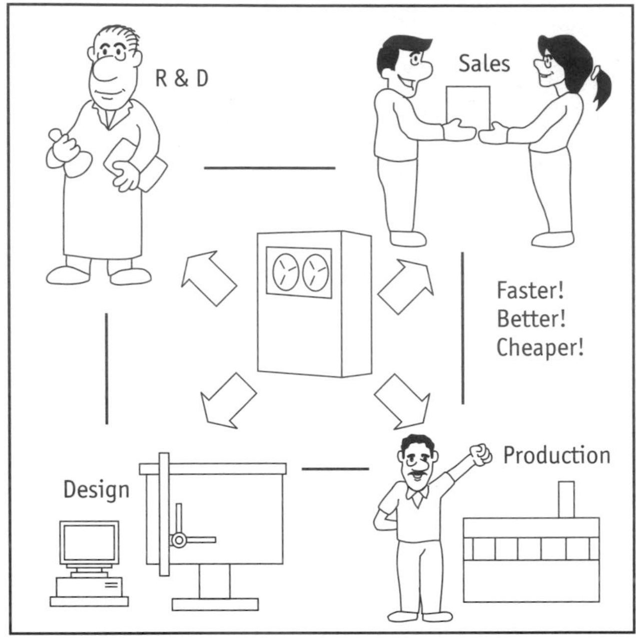

Now that the POP system is fully in place, bar code readers and sensors have eliminated the paperwork in tracking production data, freeing up time for equipment operators who previously had to hand-record their log data.

Numerical data relating to production efficiency, defect rates, and production flow can be accessed from the POP system at any time and in any part of the company. This helps the various people concerned identify problems and make quick responses.

An online system is now in place for equipment maintenance management. With little or no paperwork, equipment managers can track equipment performance and predict and prevent breakdowns.

The level-four company's CIM system enables people in product development, manufacturing, sales, and other departments to communicate and share information via computer. The database keeps everyone current with the latest production indicators, which helps the various departments work smoothly together to avoid and resolve problems concerning production, quality, or delivery.

Corrective Action to Get to Level Five

Expand 20 Keys implementation to include all sales and retail distribution employees.

To establish a companywide strategic information system (SIS), all employees in the direct and indirect departments, and even in frontline sales and retail distribution, must be aligned toward common goals and committed to implementing the 20 Keys approach. This works best if the company has reached or nearly reached level five (the "all-weather system") in Key 2, rationalizing the system/management of objectives. When a company has reached this level of implementation, any changes in the business environment, supply and demand, or conditions for achieving targets can be identified and responded to quickly by everyone in the company—from the head-office strategists and product developers to the staff in manufacturing, distribution, and sales.

A level-five company can adapt quickly to change, whether or not it has fully implemented an SIS.

Important Point

- All departments should reach level four or five in the other 19 keys.

Level Five

The CIM system has been completely implemented.

The SIS has been fine-tuned to meet the needs of the company.

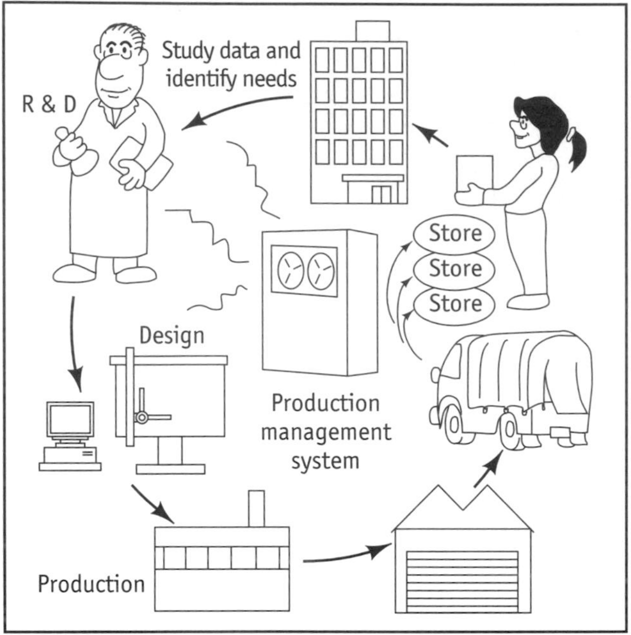

The level-five company has completed the implementation of the CIM system that was put into operation at level four, and now all manufacturing-related information has been integrated to facilitate smooth and efficient production management.

The level-five company has also fine-tuned its SIS to support the company's market-in approach toward developing appealing products that meet the latest customer needs. The frontline sales staff reports sales information to the SIS daily and the information is immediately available to and used by the R&D, design, and production planning staffs.

Any company that has reached level five in using fully integrated information systems has established a distinctive and solid edge over the competition.

Key 19

Conserving Energy and Materials

Using new and existing technologies to conserve energy and materials.

Since the oil crises of the 1970s, companies around the world have paid keen attention to the need to conserve energy and materials. In some industries, the ability to conserve these resources has been essential for survival. Recently, companies have also become more aware of the need to reduce industrial waste by recycling and by developing products that take less energy and raw materials to make.

For factories, reducing costs is an important means of ensuring profitability. Breaking down costs by section or department and setting waste-reduction goals for each group can greatly reduce manufacturing costs. At most factories, however, workers and managers are preoccupied with mishaps and snags in the production flow and tend to put energy conservation on the back burner, where it is likely to remain for weeks or months.

Although new technologies and new production equipment will help conserve energy and materials, before taking this step companies should enlist company-wide employee cooperation in making incremental improvements in energy and material conservation. A lot can be improved, even with older equipment and methods. People often fail to recognize the many energy-saving opportunities that surround them.

The first step is to quantify and report costs (including shares of total unit costs) and to emphasize the importance of conservation. Once the company has launched an energy/materials conservation campaign, improvement teams can focus their activities on this theme by making energy- or material-saving improvements. Improvements developed by teams can then be expanded as concrete conservation measures for the entire factory.

Level One

Nobody is really concerned about conserving energy and materials.

Most factories are busy, high-stress work environments. Level-one factory workers and managers are usually so busy dealing with production problems such as delivery delays and quality complaints from customers that they have little time to think about measures to conserve energy and materials. In fact, many factories have not even taken the first step of analyzing the cost of wasted resources.

The fact that there are so many problems to distract people from the issue of energy conservation is a sign of poor manufacturing quality.

Factories that use large amounts of energy and/or materials, such as forges and casting plants, have been forced to implement conservation measures to remain competitive. However, at factories that use relatively little of these resources, such as precision machining plants, people have not taken up conservation and have thereby allowed the company to lose the competitive edge it could enjoy by saving energy and materials wherever possible.

Corrective Action to Get to Level Two

Determine the share of energy and materials costs in each product's total costs.

Break costs down by section or department.

In some industries, energy and materials costs make up a large share of the total cost of finished products. When this is the case, it is especially important to quantify these costs and share the information with all employees. People can than start to become more cost-conscious and more appreciative of the positive effects (including higher profitability) that energy and material conservation can bring.

Manufacturing companies that have yet to seriously address the issue of energy conservation cannot consider themselves competitive companies with high manufacturing quality. Drastic changes in demand levels are an imminent threat, if not a reality, for many manufacturers, and those that do not have the manufacturing quality to adapt to such changes are less likely to survive the competition in their industry.

It is inexcusable for employees in staff and clerical departments to be less concerned than their colleagues in the direct (manufacturing) departments about saving energy and materials. The first step in raising energy-consciousness is to break down costs by each section or department in the company.

Important Points

- Write and disseminate in-house information on ways to conserve energy and materials.
- Clearly break down costs by section or department.

Level Two

A companywide conservation campaign has begun.

At the level-two company, a companywide conservation campaign has made everyone aware of the need to save energy and materials. Energy and materials costs have been quantified and publicized as percentages of total product costs. This campaign has also made employees more aware of the need to reduce costs in general.

By now, conservation of energy and materials has become a common theme for improvement teams and a topic of everyday conversation throughout the company. There is a new atmosphere at the company as managers and employees at all levels sense the importance of conservation to cut costs.

This campaign to cut energy and material costs is just one part of a comprehensive campaign to reduce waste of all kinds, including defect production waste and motion waste.

Corrective Action to Get to Level Three

Look around for ways to reduce energy and material consumption.

Now that the conservation campaign has raised employee awareness of energy and materials costs and improvement teams groups are working on conservation improvement projects, some employees have become eager to help but do not know where to start.

The best place to start is at home—your immediate surroundings in the workplace. Even seemingly trivial improvements, such as turning off room lights during the lunch break or using pencils and erasers until they are no longer usable, can have a significant impact on energy and material costs. You can also save energy by reducing the number or wattage of light bulbs in unnecessarily bright areas.

Study the ways energy and materials are currently used in the factory and look into ways to reduce their consumption. You may pick up valuable tips by touring a factory that is running similar equipment or processes and has made greater progress in energy and material conservation.

Important Point

- Become more knowledgeable about energy and material conservation.

Level Three

The company is cutting energy and material costs as much as possible for the existing equipment.

In foundries, whenever the doors to the forge are opened, a substantial amount of heat escapes as waste. In response to this problem, some foundry workers have measured the minimum door opening dimensions required for inserting and removing workpieces and have reduced the opening to reduce waste heat emissions.

In addition, recognizing that the forge temperature drops during hammer changeovers, these foundry workers managed to achieve single changeover and thereby raised the forge's operating rate while reducing the amount of energy consumed per kilogram of product.

Not only that, the workers found a way to reduce the thickness of the flash to increase the yield from the materials—another conservation measure that translates directly to lower product costs.

Factories should also consider the many ways to reduce water and air consumption to save resource costs.

Corrective Action to Get to Level Four

Establish companywide or section-based conservation goals.

Make full use of existing technology to reduce consumption.

To get to level four, the company must tie its various separate conservation projects into a coordinated, factorywide approach. Set concrete goals, such as reducing energy consumption 20 percent and raising the yield 10 percent, and use graphs to track progress toward achieving these goals.

The company will also need to involve others besides the improvement teams and must find room in the budget to modify equipment and make other necessary changes to reduce energy and material consumption. Shortening processes is one obvious way to cut energy costs. Analyze the current production system to see whether any processes or process steps contain large amounts of waste and can be shortened, perhaps by adopting a different technology.

Reading up on energy conservation case studies from other companies can also reveal some specific methods that can be used in your own company.

Important Point

- Establish and promote quantified goals.

Level Four

A comprehensive companywide conservation program is in place and some improvements have been achieved already.

While the level-three company has made conservation improvements centered on improvement team activities and limited to inexpensive projects, the level-four company has developed an integrated, comprehensive conservation program by which it can set priorities among conservation needs from a companywide perspective. When necessary, the level-four company can appropriate funds for resource-saving equipment modifications.

For example, lining furnace exteriors with ceramic tile is one way to reduce waste heat. Another approach is installation of heat exchangers that use the hot combustion exhaust to heat the secondary air returned to the combustion chamber. Concrete equipment modification measures such as these are being devised and implemented throughout the factory.

Other conservation efforts at this level include measures to increase material yield by recycling scrap into material that can still be used for making products. Reducing defects also helps increase material yield, which is why good quality assurance is essential for minimizing industrial wastes.

Corrective Action to Get to Level Five

Thoroughly pursue conservation in minor and major ways.

Develop new technologies that conserve resources.

Take a zero-based cost-budgeting perspective.

Having reached level four, the company has made all possible conservation improvements that use only existing technology or borrow ideas learned from plant visits or case studies of other factories. To make further progress, the company must now develop and implement new conservation technologies.

For example, automotive engine designers have used microprocessors to control the supply of fuel and air to car engines as a means of increasing fuel efficiency. Although this is an example of a technology that helps product users save energy, the same principle of conservation applies to product manufacturers as well.

Important Points

- Develop and use new technologies.
- Recycle materials to reduce industrial waste.

Level Five

The company meets its conservation goals while developing and using new technology.

An extensive recycling program reduces industrial waste.

The level-five company, with its comprehensive conservation program, has enacted measures to achieve all of its conservation goals and has developed new technologies for saving energy and materials. For example, a level-five foundry is able to expertly control and conserve its forge heat from quenching to tempering to realize significant energy savings.

As another example, consider a level-five factory that makes rotating vanes and turbochargers. Rather than using expensive heat-resistant alloys for the entire rotating vane, this factory found they could use these alloys on just the areas exposed to extreme heat and use less costly regular steel in cooler areas such as the axle. They used electron-beam welding to weld the vane parts together.

Other level-five factories have found ways to recycle water to conserve resources and save money.

The level-five company also realizes that conservation improvements are never-ending: there are always new techniques to be developed to conserve resources and reduce industrial waste.

Key 20

Leading Technology and Site Technology

The application of technology based on companywide awareness.

Leading technology and site technology are evaluated differently from the other keys, which are scored according to factory-floor conditions. Instead, the entire company is evaluated on the application of technology and on its position in relation to its competition.

Site technology is the set of skills, knowledge, and devices that the people in a company acquire as they develop their processes. It is an intangible asset that does not necessarily increase when new equipment is introduced. Rather, it is what enables a company to function strategically and ensure competitiveness by making the best use of new equipment in a short time. With today's ever shorter product life cycles, the ability to switch over to a new product rapidly and smoothly—a function of site technology—is increasingly important. However, site technology rests with the people who have developed it. Therefore it is also very important to have a system for transferring site technology to newer workers while encouraging each new generation of workers to add its own improvements.

Today, many companies are betting their futures on the development of new technologies, including integrated circuits and electronic machinery. Appropriate use of new technology can spell success or failure, especially in developing industries. New and existing technologies should be interwoven like a strong fabric. The strength of site technology can be seen in the speed with which the company is able to successfully incorporate new technology.

Every company should be aware of how its technology compares to that of its competitors. Is your company at the top of your industry or is it in a lower class? Carefully consider the areas where your technology is lagging and plan measures to catch up. Leading companies cannot afford to be complacent: a technological edge can be lost in a matter of months. These days, new technologies do not remain new for long.

Level One

Not even interested in monitoring the technological progress of its competitors, the company is content with its current technology.

Justly proud of their attainments using technology, some people think that their established technology is all they need to ensure future success as well. In this sense, pride has blinded people to the need for new technology to remain truly competitive.

No matter how successful their technology has been, factory managers must consider some tough questions:

- Does the company's technology lead the industry or has the company already fallen behind the competition?
- Will sticking with existing technology enable the factory to grow or will it more likely cause it to shrink?
- Are some departments way ahead of others? Do they have a methodology for updating skills and passing on knowledge?

The level-one company is like the hare in "The Tortoise and the Hare"—too complacent and self-assured to keep an eye out for the competition. In these fast-changing times, companies must remember the moral of this story: if you snooze, you lose.

Level Two

The company recognizes that it is relatively slow to adopt new technologies.

It is often difficult to determine when a company is at level two, but when a company suddenly realizes that it is about to be overrun by more technologically advanced competitors, that's a beginning.

Level-two companies that are not so severely threatened by the competition nevertheless recognize the areas in which they are weak and are motivated to further improve their technology and accelerate their adoption of leading technologies.

Once a company realizes it is at level two and understands the significance of this condition, it is already on the road to level three.

The level-two company must realize that if it remains at level two for long, it will almost certainly be overtaken and beaten by its competitors. Managers and employees should recognize that their efforts to get to level three and beyond are a life-and-death struggle for the company's future.

Level Three

The company is keeping pace technologically with the average for the industry.

Some companies subjectively assess themselves against their competition on the basis of limited information. They do not understand how their competitors reach their results, and they are satisfied if they are as good as the average. This is a sign of complacency: managers feel that if the company sticks to what it is doing now, they will succeed. This attitude precludes any kind of passion for improvement making.

The level three company visits trade fairs, analyzes competitors' products to figure out how they built them, benchmarks its technology against its competitors', and implements training and development to ensure that its staff are continually brought up to date. Level three companies have sufficient capability to export their products and compete in foreign markets.

When scoring your company, score separately for your position in relation to your competitors and for the way you develop your staff to ensure that they are continually updated in the application of technology.

Level Four

The company is one step ahead of the industry average.

The company is able to successfully incorporate new technologies.

The level-four factory has established an edge over the average factory in its industry, but it must keep working at the same types of issues it confronted at level three.

The company has introduced internal and external benchmarking. Externally, it recognizes the limitations of comparisons within its own industry. It looks at the very best products and processes wherever they occur, transferring these lessons to its own business. Managers recognize that new advances appear in the marketplace every day and change constantly, so they continually review and upgrade the criteria by which they assess the company's competence.

Internally, the company ensures that new technology is applied across the company, with departments and functions cross-fertilizing and learning from each other.

Level Five

The company's site technology is among the best in the industry.

The company monitors and performs at the leading edge in basic and new technologies related to its business.

The level-five factory is preeminent both in its site technologies and in its ability to maintain technological progress by adopting and developing new technologies. This leadership position helps boost morale and confidence to an all-time high. However, the race is not over—like a marathon runner, the factory cannot afford to become complacent even if it is in the lead. The competition is always fiercest at the leading edge, so the factory must continue its benchmarking and competitive analysis to maintain and improve its level-five position.

It takes both speed and endurance to win a long race. This is also true in the competition among companies to develop their site technologies and leading technologies. The company's ability to apply new technology and its progress in all 20 Keys ensure that the company performs well in all measures of competitive success.

Advice for Improvement at Levels 3, 4, and 5

Identify and pursue the important technologies in each department.

Develop new, leading technologies to revolutionize site technology.

Identify the technologies needed by your department, then rate your department relative to the world's best competitors. Make sure everyone knows your rating.

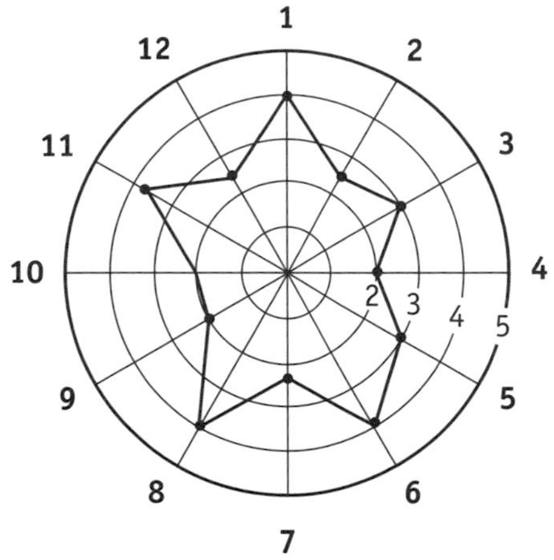

1 2 3 4 5 6 7 8 9 10 11 12

2 3 4 5

The numbers around this radar chart represent the technologies needed by the department.

Conduct a survey in each department, asking employees to name the most important technologies for their department. Organize the responses and make a list of key technologies for each department. Then rate each department's position in each technology relative to the entire industry and inform the department employees of their position.

Next, make a radar chart based on these results. This chart will provide a framework for refining site technology and developing leading technology and is useful for encouraging focused efforts in certain areas. Use the radar chart to determine which technology requires attention first and enact specific measures directed at each technology needing improvement.

Advice for Improvement at Levels 3, 4, and 5 (continued)

Make sure that each generation further develops the site technology.

Establish a system for passing site technology from generation to generation.

Improvements in site technology and leading technology can never be short-term projects. Strength, endurance, and ongoing education are required to support technological improvements as long-term projects within the company's long-term business plan.

20 Keys Matrix

Target Key: Key 20–Leading Technology and Site Technology

Countermeasures for related keys to help improve the target key.	
1. Cleaning and organizing	Post technology training charts to encourage technology improvement.
2. Rationalizing the system/ management of objectives	Introduce new technologies to support accumulation of high-quality site technology.
3. Improvement teams	Adopt new technologies, then have teams adapt them for even better site technologies.
4. Reducing inventory	Introduce new technologies to help establish one-piece flow and zero inventory.
5. Quick changeover	Gather knowledge gained from devising quick changeover as site technology.
6. Manufacturing value analysis	Refine productivity-boosting techniques as site technologies.
7. Zero monitor manufacturing	Gather know-how on zero monitoring and one-page standards as site technologies.
8. Coupled manufacturing	Gather know-how on process connections and on staff communication as site technologies.
9. Maintaining equipment	Introduce new technologies to improve equipment reliability.
10. Time control and commitment	Start study groups for people interested in learning about new technologies.
11. Quality assurance system	Develop new technologies to help reach zero defects.
12. Developing your suppliers	Provide guidance and support to suppliers who are introducing new technologies.
13. Eliminating waste (treasure map)	Devise ways to completely eliminate waste from current processes before introducing new automation technologies.
14. Empowering workers	Gather knowledge gained from making improvements as site technology.
15. Skill versatility and cross-training	Use cross-training as a means of further refining site technologies.
16. Production scheduling	Make use of process scheduling know-how when introducing new production management techniques.
17. Efficiency control	Use efficiency control to determine cost-effectiveness of new equipment investments.
18. Using information systems	Stay abreast of new microprocessor applications and develop uses based on site technologies.
19. Conserving energy and materials	Gather know-how on energy- and resource-saving improvements as site technologies.
20. Leading technology/ site technology	

Postscript

Implementing the 20 Keys

The book has described the 20 Keys individually and has shown how factories can quantify their current level in each key and can plan and enact corrective actions to get to higher levels. At this point, I would like to stress the importance of the synergistic interaction of these 20 Keys and how the keys can be implemented in various combinations and sequences for the greatest effect.

The 20 Keys approach is a practical program for synergistically combining "foothold" improvements in various interrelated keys so that your factory can produce high-quality products more quickly, inexpensively, and easily than ever before. The 20 Keys system shows companies how to tailor a concrete, practical implementation program to suit their own needs and conditions, the overall objective being factory "revolution" (as seen in productivity doubling, lead time halving, and the elimination of quality complaints). No matter whether the plant uses mass-production or a wide-variety, small-lot production, or what industry or country it is in, it can revolutionize itself by implementing the 20 Keys. This system also applies to nonmanufacturing activities, from product planning, development, and design to engineering, sales, product servicing, and various kinds of management activities.

Take another look at the 20 Keys Relations Diagram pictured on page 2. Note once again that Key 1 (cleaning and organizing), Key 2 (rationalizing the system/management of objectives), Key 3 (improvement team activities), and Key 20 (leading technology/site technology) constitute the four outside corners of this diagram. They are placed as cornerstones to underscore their role as fundamental building blocks of the 20 Keys system.

Key 1 (cleaning and organizing) is where everything starts—and it is never too early or too late to start. The program not only starts with Key 1, it returns to Key 1 for reevaluation after the factory has made some progress in other keys and again as it nears level five in all other keys, to ensure that the fundamental support of cleaning and organizing is being maintained.

The main function of Key 2 (rationalizing the system/management of objectives) is to help managers and shopfloor supervisors unify their approach and align their vectors in pursuing goals. No matter what combination of keys your factory is pursuing, this remains an essential one.

Key 3 (improvement team activities) is fundamental as the mechanism by which all employees join forces to strengthen the factory's manufacturing quality by pursuing improvement goals.

Key 20 (leading technology/site technology) underlies all of the other keys inasmuch as improvements in any of the other keys tie in with improvement in leading technology and/or site technology. Conversely, improvements in Key 20 foster improvements in all other keys.

Note also that arrows are drawn from certain keys to the essential manufacturing characteristics in the center of the diagram to which they are most closely related. Key 11 (quality assurance system) points toward "Better," while Key 6 (manufacturing value analysis) and Key 19 (conserving energy and materials) point toward "Cheaper" and Key 4 (reducing inventory) points toward "Faster." Therefore, a factory might aim to achieve level three in Key 11 to cut the defect rate by half, level three in Key 4 to reduce inventory by half (or level 4 to reduce it by 75 percent), and level four in Key 6 to reduce labor-hours by half (such as by doubling productivity).

While considering such special emphases, remember that all keys are related to the central theme of strengthening manufacturing quality, which is shown at the very center of the circle. Remember also that the 20 Keys are all interrelated and all serve as footholds on the climb to success.

The order in which the 20 Keys are implemented and the target levels in each key may differ according to where the factory is currently weakest or where it most wants to emphasize improvement, such as in reducing quality complaints, shortening production lead time, or doubling productivity to lower costs. For example, if a company's number one goal is to build manufacturing strength by doubling productivity, it would implement the 20 Keys in a way that establishes the footholds needed to reach level four in Key 6 (manufacturing value analysis).

Flow and Progress of 20 Keys Implementation

Generally, a company that has put together a 20 Keys program suited to its needs implements the program as a medium-term plan lasting about three years. It progresses through the following stages of implementation:

1. Preparation. During this stage, the company studies the 20 Keys and begins implementing Key 1 (cleaning and organizing). The company performs a

preliminary evaluation of its current levels. Even during this preliminary stage, it is possible to make real strides by making substantial improvements.

2. Introduction. This stage generally corresponds to the program's first year. Everyone learns the basics of the 20 Keys and integrates the 20 Keys approach into their daily life.
3. Promotion. This stage generally corresponds to the program's second year. During this stage, 20 Keys techniques and skills are integrated with all production activities and employees hone their techniques while pursuing ever more ambitious improvement activities.
4. Full development. 20 Keys techniques and improvement activities are a solid part of the corporate culture, and have enabled the company to achieve the goal of doubling productivity.

Stages of 20 Keys Implementation

Stages	Preparation	Introduction	Promotion	Full Development	Further Expansion
Time Frame	9 months to 1 year	First year	Second year	Third year	Fourth year onward
Events	▼ Introductory lectures	▼ Kickoff			
Multilevel meetings	▼ First meeting	▼ Midterm meeting ▼ Second meeting	▼ Midterm meeting ▼ Third meeting	▼ Midterm meeting ▼ Fourth meeting	▼ ▼
Productivity UP target		30%	30%	30% Doubled in three years: receive bronze medal	30% Tripled in six years: receive silver medal

Self-Evaluation

After a factory has been running its production in a certain way for a long time, people tend not to think about ways they could change things to build manufacturing strength. Stability leads to complacency.

The first step in revolutionizing a factory is to determine with some precision where the factory stands in relation to its competitors around the world. Once you recognize your current position, you are better able to devise short-, medium-, and long-term plans for making improvements and reaching goals.

It is also a good idea to determine the 20 Keys rating of the entire company. Hold an assembly for the entire company (or for the middle and upper managers if the company is too large) and explain the meaning of the 20 Keys and the five-level scoring system, using illustrations such as the relations diagram. Then have each person fill out a scoring sheet anonymously.

Many people are reluctant to admit areas where their company is inferior to competitors in the same country or region, which makes it hard to get an accurate self-evaluation. That is why companies should compare themselves not to their local competitors but rather to manufacturing companies in all industries all over the world.

Once people see a score that ranks their company or factory among other companies or factories, they become more aware of their company's weaknesses and are more easily motivated to overcome them. When everyone suddenly becomes conscious of the need for improvement, you may be surprised at how quickly a new spirit of zeal arises.

The 20 Keys Kickoff

Post action plans in each department and hold large assembly-type meetings to help kick off the 20 Keys campaign. Many companies choose to time their kickoff events in sync with the start of their business year.

Multilevel Meetings

1. Hold the first multilevel meetings one or two months before the 20 Keys kickoff events.
2. Hold a daylong meeting that includes everyone from top managers to shopfloor workers (or their representatives).
3. Using Key 2's vector alignment sheets, align vectors concerning quantified goals to establish a common approach toward goal achievement.
4. After a month or two, set up a three-point program (the three points are "basic factory policy," "goal achievement image," and "revolutionary program") for the next year.

Action Plans

Use the three-point program described above as a basis for drafting detailed implementation plans (monthly action plans) for each key, using action plan forms. Set numerical target values and write down who is responsible for doing what by when. These action plans will be used later to help manage daily improvement activities. Post the action plan in the workplace so anyone can check it easily at any time.

Monitoring Improvement Activities

Using the 20 Keys action plan forms, keep track of implementation progress from month to month. Use arrows to indicate items that have been implemented and use a graphic technique (such as bar charts) to indicate the degree to which targets have been reached and the corresponding percentages. Review these progress charts at the midterm multilevel meetings held every half year to get a clearer view of what must still be done to meet year-end goals.

PPORF Prizes

The PPORF Development Institute has established awards given to companies that achieve various degrees of progress in revolutionizing their factories and strengthening their manufacturing quality through the 20 Keys. The table below lists the three PPORF prizes and the criteria for awarding them.

PPORF Prizes		In an enviroment of global recession and declining sales and profits in the industry.		
	Score	Sales	Profits	Status (comment)
Bronze medal	65 points; solidly above 60 points	↘	→	Profits do not shrink even when total revenues decline.
Silver medal	75 points; solidly above 70 points	→	↗	Sales do not decline, and profits increase
Gold medal	85 points; solidly above 80 points	↗	↗	Sales and profits are both increasing

Following the sequence of steps just described, each company makes a companywide effort, linking top-down decision making with bottom-up suggestions, to create plans for implementing the 20 Keys. Next, they monitor implementation progress, using graphs and other visual management tools to keep everyone informed of current conditions. When goals are reached, everyone is excited, knowing they have been part of the effort from the start.

Improvement Case Study

The chart below tracks several trends during one company's first three years of 20 Keys implementation: scores in the keys, productivity rates, and staffing levels in indirect departments.

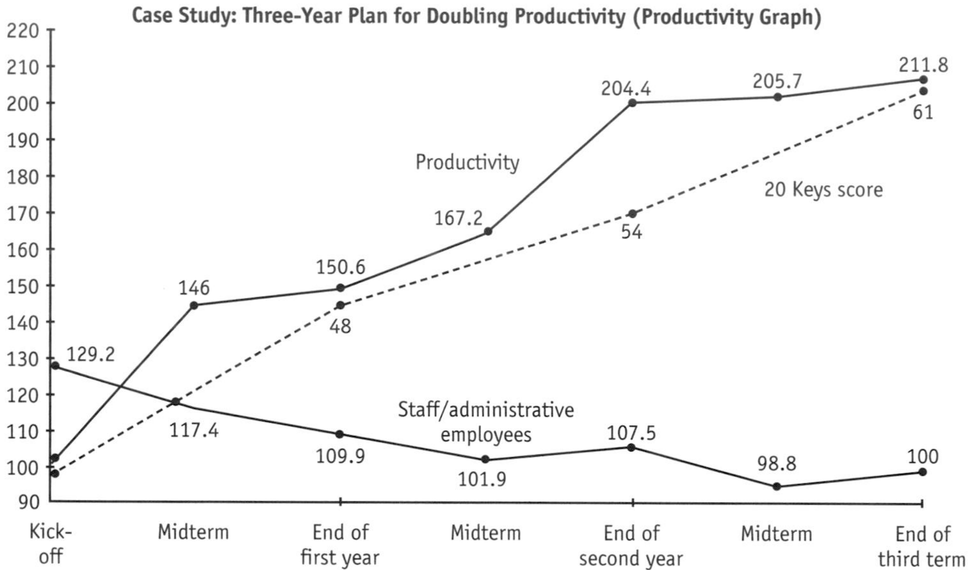

This company was facing an urgent need to boost productivity so as to remain competitive on the domestic market, which had been experiencing a shift toward moving production overseas. Consequently, their implementation plan emphasized raising productivity. Within two years, the company raised its overall 20 Keys score by 17 points and doubled productivity. During the third year, the company started establishing new footholds toward other types of goals, and therefore its productivity gains were small, but its overall score (indicating overall manufacturing quality) grew steadily higher.

As for the third trend, overall staffing levels in indirect departments shrank about 30 percent over the three years even though sales grew by 50 percent. This meant a doubling of the amount of sales (i.e., business) handled by the average indirect department employee. Improvements in indirect departments contributed greatly toward shortening production lead time. The indirect department employees at this company can proudly share with the manufacturing employees a sense of accomplishment for having produced these remarkable results.

20 Keys Activities in Indirect Departments

As in the case study just described, more and more indirect departments are helping to revolutionize their companies through the 20 Keys approach system. The chart below shows a few of the ways in which indirect departments can take part in 20 Keys implementation.

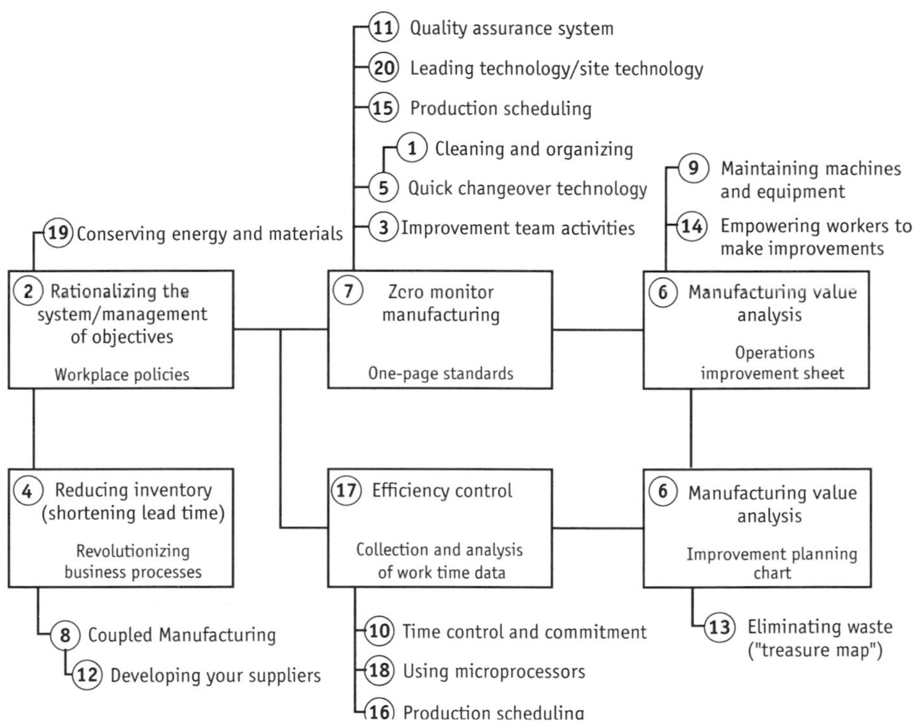

For indirect departments, the first step in improvement making is to clarify what each section or department is expected to do. If there is confusion on this point, improvement projects are not likely to get anywhere. The work begins with using categories set under the "functional deployment of work duties" as the basis for creating new workplace regulations that will help improve Key 2 (rationalizing the system/management of objectives). Next, write and adopt one-page standards for work procedures to make progress toward zero monitoring (Key 7).

Then, using the work elements described in the one-page standards, fill out operation improvement sheets to plan improvements that will cut labor-hours and raise work efficiency. Finally, using the various categories of work regulations as a basis, create a daily work record on which labor-hours and output can be tracked for the sake of efficiency control (Key 17).

The knowledge of work procedures embodied in one-page standards becomes a tool for implementing skill versatility and cross-training (Key 15) and for passing down leading technology and site technology (Key 20). Since one-page standards help to eliminate human errors, they also support the improvement of the quality assurance system (Key 11) and strengthen clerical operations.

Using the handbook for reducing inventory (Key 4) that is based on the company's work regulations, implement rule number one—studying the current production flow—and then create stores as a device for coupled manufacturing (Key 8). Also, apply the fishbowl discussion method to remove barriers between departments and then redesign the work processes. Use single trays to reduce clerical work-in-process (Key 4), which in turn will help reduce lead time and labor-hours.

The 20 Keys and ISO 9000

Recently, a number of companies that are implementing the 20 Keys system have received certification under the ISO 9001 and ISO 9002 standards. Although the ISO 9000 family of standards falls mainly within the domain of implementing Key 11 (quality assurance system), it relates to many other keys as well. Implementation of the 20 Keys helps companies prepare for and receive ISO certification. The following keys are related specifically to ISO 9000 certification:

- Key 2 (rationalizing the system/management of objectives): work regulations that organize and clearly define realms of responsibility.
- Key 7 (zero monitor manufacturing): one-page standards help clarify and smooth the flow of work.
- Key 5 (quick changeover technology): the "single file" system speeds up retrieval of documents and other information.
- Key 1 (cleaning and organizing): overall cleanliness and orderliness in the workplace and clear sorting out of nonconforming products (rejects).

Naturally, the keys that tie in with ISO 9000 certification are those that deal with quality-related duties, procedures, or standards. Because the 20 Keys system incorporates these issues, a company does not need to establish a separate program in addition to 20 Keys implementation to prepare its quality system for an ISO audit.

In addition to the direct advantages already described, implementation of the 20 Keys system works quickly to establish a common approach at all levels of the company, thereby creating a stronger impetus toward achieving goals such as combining top-down decision-making with bottom-up suggestions and obtaining ISO 9000 certification.

When undergoing any kind of external audit, companies that have implemented Key 1's cleaning and organizing and Key 5's single-file system are sure to impress auditors with the appearance of their facilities and with their speed in providing requested information.

Summary

In conclusion, I would note that although the illustrations in this book relate mainly to machine shops, foundries, sheet metal processing plants, and assembly plants, with fewer sentences related to offices and other indirect departments, the 20 Keys system can be applied to any kind of enterprise. Also, it is important to remember that the meaning of numerical scores must be adjusted to suit your particular factory or other workplace. Once you have defined these scores according to your own circumstances, start making progress in one-point or half-point increments. Periodically review the definitions and adjust them again if necessary. As you gain experience in implementing the 20 Keys system, it will be easier to define your scores and to understand and achieve your objectives.

The overall objective for everyone is to make progress point by point, working toward the twofold goal of raising your total score by 20 points and doubling productivity. The result will be the transformation of your company into a strong, change-adaptive manufacturer.

Appendix A

The Fishbowl Discussion Method

The fishbowl discussion method was invented by the PPORF Development Institute as a forum for related departments in an organization to use for listening to requests and expressing opinions openly. The purpose is to solve problems and plan future improvements by listening closely and with an open mind.

During a discussion, when one group of people hears another group saying something that is disadvantageous to the first group or opposite to their own opinion, they tend to start refuting it while the other group is still talking. When this happens, the other group cannot communicate their interests and demands fully. The discussion often gets off the track due to people's reactions.

The fishbowl discussion method was designed to avoid this situation by encouraging two or more groups to listen carefully to each other and absorb what the others are saying.

In this method, members of the participating groups are seated in two concentric circles (see diagram). The group in the inner circle is "in the fishbowl" and is called the "goldfish group." During their turn in the fishbowl they are not allowed to respond while people in the other group are speaking. Instead, they listen carefully and take notes about what is said. After the discussion, the groups organize their notes, think about solutions to the issues raised, and take action to improve the situation.

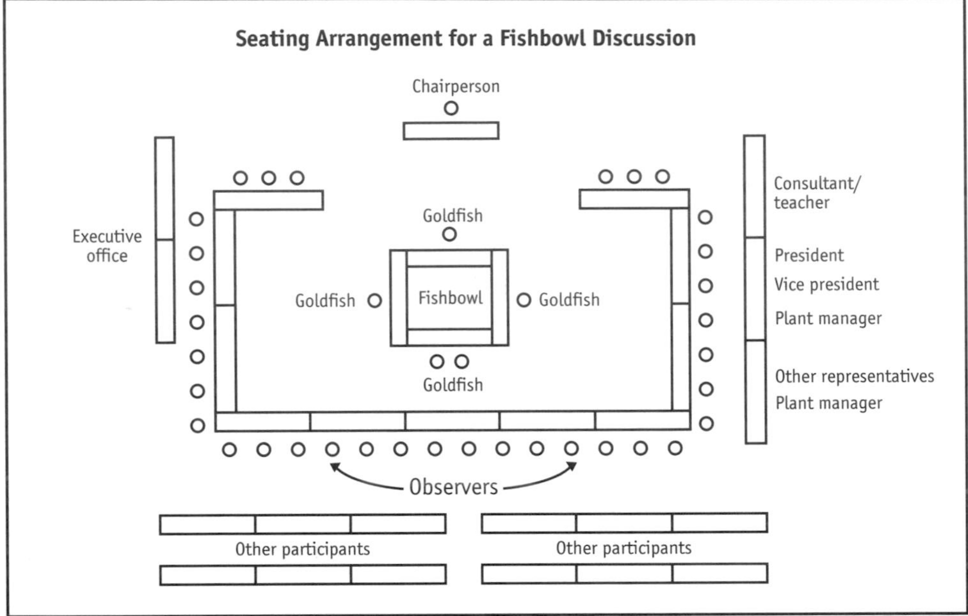

Around the outside circle sit the "observers." Members of this group are recognized in turn to express their observations, opinions, and ideas to the goldfish group without interruption.

This process is intended to include managers as well as other employees in the departments. Someone from the executive office should serve as the chairperson.

The participating groups take turns as goldfish and as observer/speakers until everyone has had a chance to speak.

The observer group follows these groundrules:

- A person who wants to speak must raise a hand. He or she may speak when recognized by the chairperson. The speaker begins by stating his or her name and department.
- Others may not talk while the speaker is talking.
- The speaker must prepare what he or she wants to say, and speak clearly and briefly.
- Other observers may comment on the speaker by raising a hand and waiting for recognition from the chairperson. They may speak as many times as they want.
- Each speaker has a one-minute limit, after which the floor is granted to another person. Speakers rotate, so that the discourse is not dominated by two people.

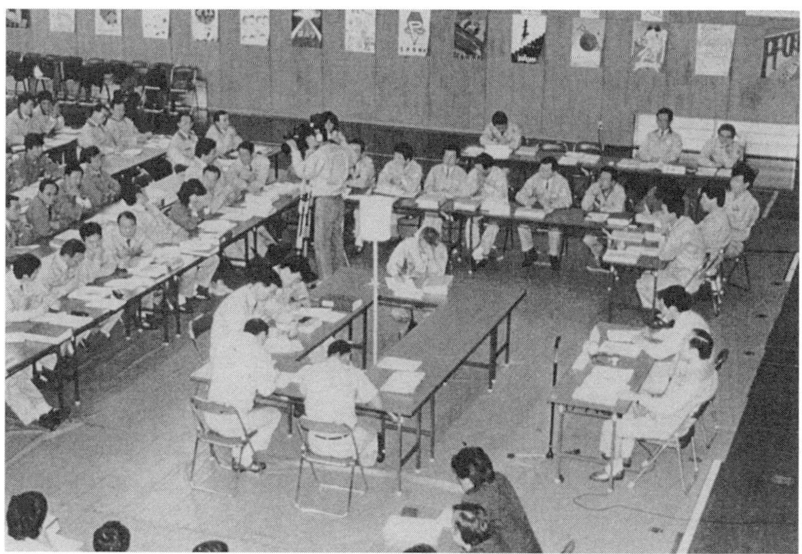

A fishbowl discussion at Morioka Seiko Works (photo courtesy of Morioka Seiko, Ltd. and NKS)

For their part, the goldfish in the middle select one person as a notetaker to record everything said by the observer group members. They listen carefully and with an open mind. After all the opinions are presented, each group leader offers solutions to the problems raised if they can be resolved right away. If the problems require further work to resolve, each group takes the questions and issues back to the workplace, discusses it further, and reports answers later to the executive office, which in turn informs the other groups.

Appendix B — Charts and Figures

Supplement to Key 7

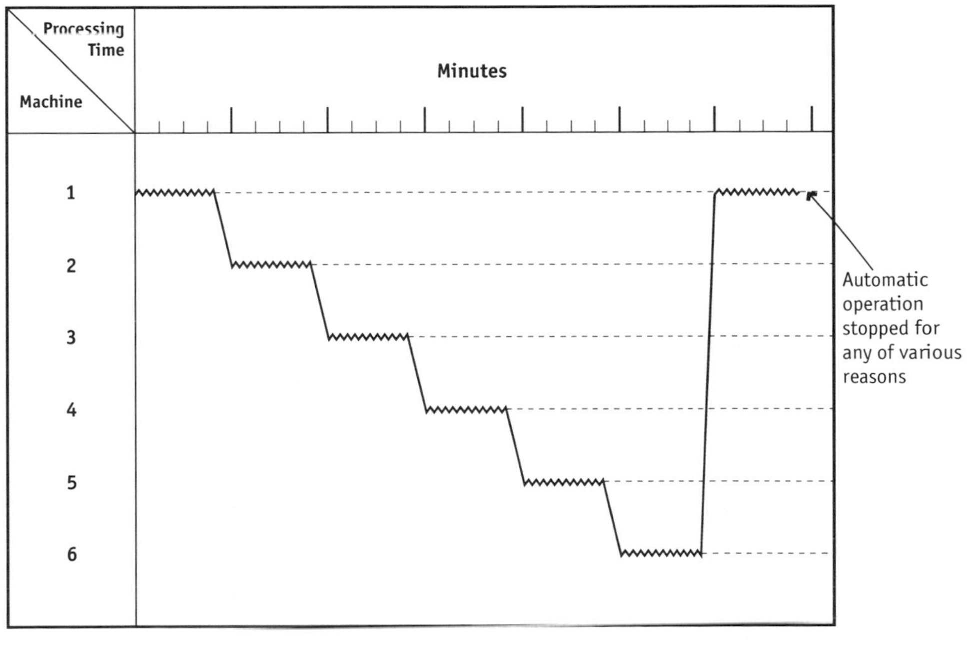

Supplement to Key 6

Operations Improvement Sheet — General Operations

Object: Making it easier to take apart the intake pump Date: 5/15/90

No.	Task	Cum. Time	Time	Real Work	Waste					Problem Areas	Corrective Action	Time Savings	Responsible	Action Date
					Trans-port	Walk-ing	Watch-ing	Search-ing	Other					
1	Putting the pump on the workbench		180		√	√		√		Because there is no specified work table, time is spent search-ing for a place to work.	A pump work cart would avoid the search time.	30		8/30
2	Gathering the tools	360	180			√		√		Can't easily find the tools to use.	Leave tools on the dedicated work cart.	0		"
3	Preparing the parts for use	840	480		√	√		√		Too much walking around and carrying things.	Prepare necessary parts in advance.	0	NM	9/30
4	Removing fixtures	960	120	√						Used a box wrench to take it off.	Switch to an impact wrench.	60		6/30
5	Removing cylinder pipe	1089	129	√						Pump not tied down, moves around.	Use a clamp to fix the pump to the work cart.	100		"
6	Removing piston packing	1218	129	√						"	"	110		"

Supplement to Key 5

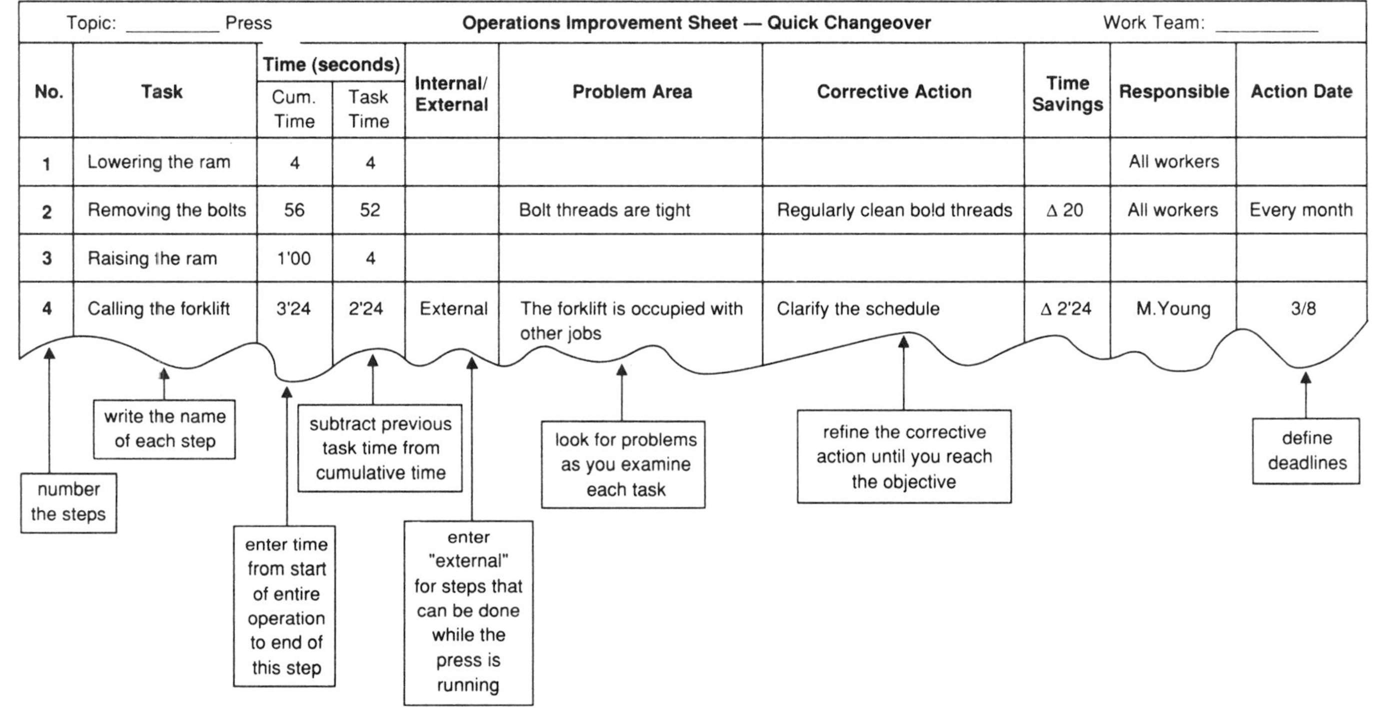

Topic: _________ Press — Operations Improvement Sheet — Quick Changeover — Work Team: __________

No.	Task	Time (seconds)		Internal/ External	Problem Area	Corrective Action	Time Savings	Responsible	Action Date
		Cum. Time	Task Time						
1	Lowering the ram	4	4					All workers	
2	Removing the bolts	56	52		Bolt threads are tight	Regularly clean bold threads	Δ 20	All workers	Every month
3	Raising the ram	1'00	4						
4	Calling the forklift	3'24	2'24	External	The forklift is occupied with other jobs	Clarify the schedule	Δ 2'24	M.Young	3/8

Supplement to Key 13

Treasure Map

Round: 9

Sampling Period: Sept. 1-30, 1988

Objective: Actual work greater than 85%

Gold — Silver — Copper — In order, from highest waste to the lowest.

Gold Mine Actual Work: Up to 70% of average
Waste Work: More than 125% of average

Silver Mine Actual Work: Up to 80% of average
Waste Work: Up to 125% of average

Copper Mine Actual Work: Up to 100% of average
Waste Work: Up to 110% of average

Flatlands Actual Work: Greater than average
Waste Work: Less than average

Detail	Groups (Indirect Depts.)	Energy Conservation Mgmt./ Engrs.	Fabrication Mgmt./ Engrs.	Roll Design	Shipping Mgmt.	Engineering Office	General Affairs	Electronics	Mfg. Engineering							Aver. of Indirect Depts.
Actual Work	Average from last period	62.7	66.5	70.8	72	66.9	75.7	71.7	74.2							69.4
	Goal for this period	72.8	76.5	75	85.5	72	85	80	78							
	This period	70.2	68.9	77.8	75.5	69.6	76.2	77.2	79							73.2
	Gold/Silver/Copper															
Improvement Ratio	% Improvement	12	3.6	9.9	4.9	4	0.7	7.7	6.5							5.5
	Ranking	1	7	2	5	6	8	3	4							
Accomplishment Rate	% Accomplished	96.4	90.1	103.7	88.3	96.7	89.6	96.5	101.3							
	Ranking	5	6	1	8	3	7	4	2							
Special Awards	Greater than 85%															
	Greater than 90%															

Breakdown of Waste																
	Transporting	1.4	0.6	0.7	0.7	1.3	1.2	1.1	1.2							1
	Walk ng	3.8	3.6	1.5	3.4	3.2	1.6	3.5	4.7							3.2
	Changeover	2.2	1.2	1.3	1.3	1.3	1.1	1.6	1.8							1.5
	Searching	2.6	1.2	0.9	2.4	0.9	0.1	1.3	0.9							1.3
Watching	Time Thinking	3.5	6	4.4	1.8	1.3	2	1.8	0.6							2.9
Watching	Time Watching	0.6	1	1.7	1.1	1.2	0.7	0.7	1							1
Watching	Total	4.1	7	6.1	2.9	2.5	2.7	2.5	1.6							3.9
Talking	Telephone	4	3.3	2.1	3.9	7.7	6.3	2.5	0.8							4.2
Talking	Coordination	5.9	8.1	4.2	2.8	5.3	2.2	3.5	1.5							4.6
Talking	Business Meetings	3.2	3.2	2.2	3.7	4	3.4	3.2	3.7							3.4
Talking	Total	13.1	14.6	8.5	10.4	17	11.9	9.2	6							12.2
	Other	0.5	1	1.5	0.8	1.2	1.4	1.6	1.2							1.1
	Out o' Seat	2.1	1.9	1.7	2.6	3	3.8	2	3.6							2.6

Note: This example, provided by the author, shows an actual Treasure Map used by a company that implemented the PPORF System. The map at the top is a depiction of Honshu, the main island of Japan; any other area with diverse geographical features can be used for this purpose. —Ed.

Appendix C

Case Study: Microcomputers and 20 Keys Activities at Morioka Seiko Works*

The Seiko Electronics Watch Division kicked off its PPORF 20 Keys program in October, 1991 after a year of preparatory activities to build momentum. The division headquarters had set a target of becoming the best watch group in the world, an enterprise-wide movement that included, directly or indirectly, four domestic Japanese firms and five foreign firms, with the Morioka Seiko Works as its pilot plant. At the same time these goals were set, the firm also started a 20 Keys program. In its first year, reported here, it had already made vast groupwide improvements in all 20 Keys.

Morioka Seiko Works was established in 1970. In 1993 it was capitalized at ¥100 million and employed 1,100 people.

The following material includes an interview with the president of Morioka Seiko about the company's 20 Keys implementation, a discussion about the overall 20 Keys program, and a focused description of the implementation of Key 18, involving microprocessors.

An Interview with Akira Takaishi, President of Morioka Seiko

by Ikuo Nishiumi

Q: Tell us about the sequence of events leading up to your PPORF 20 Keys implementation.

Takaishi: We invited Director Sato of Akai Sakidama to our semiannual cooperative study meeting, and after we heard his discussion of the PPORF 20 Kcys system, Kiyoshi Ito, our vice president at the time, burst out, "Eureka!" and we decided to implement the 20 Keys in our firm.

**Adapted from articles published in* NKS Factory Magazine, *volume 39, no. 2, 1993. Used by permission.*

Although improving our productivity, increasing yield, and shortening lead times were areas we had already been working on, the QC and IE methods we had put in place still left some areas rather unclear when it came to improvements on an integrated level. The ability of the 20 Keys approach to solve this problem convinced us to implement it. Shortly thereafter I received word that we must make preparations because the program was to be deployed throughout the firm, and was to center on Morioka Seiko.

Q: Why did it start with Morioka Seiko?

Takaishi: In the watch division at that time we had already begun activities we called "WR-21" to restructure the watch division in preparation for the twenty-first century. Given the difficulty we had in recruiting manufacturing employees in the region where we were located, combined with our factory's use of two different types of manufacturing operations, Morioka Seiko was selected as the focus plant for the domestic watch manufacturing business.

At about the same time (February, 1991) we began PPORF study meetings. Morioka was selected in these meetings to be the model factory because all involved parties agreed on the goal of eliminating waste. I think that we found PPORF at a very opportune time.

Q: How has the factory changed since you implemented PPORF?

Takaishi: PPORF is a method which the employees accept because the matrix of 20 issues it deals with is well organized and because it is not difficult. Starting with the 4S's is good because they are easy to understand. Also, because we are able to quantitatively score points for the state of progress of our improvements, we can tell at a glance how we are doing.

Along with that, PPORF is good because it has shared vocabulary. We have offshore factories in Thailand, Singapore, Taiwan, Dairen (China), and Hong Kong; using the 20 Keys we can talk to each other at these plants with a shared understanding.

Q: I have heard that your initial diagnostic score was quite poor. As a new company president at that time (August, 1990), what did you think about that?

Takaishi: It wasn't that much of a shock. When I first became president I was immersed in the mood of the company as a whole. Having been appointed president at a time when there was not 100 percent trust between the company and the employees, I pondered what I should do to gain their confidence.

The first thing I thought was "let's play!" and we decided to have the company participate with its own group in the Sansa Festival, which is a major local event. We prepared matching light summer kimonos and large Japanese drums. At first those employees who didn't know me very well were startled and amazed, but soon they began to understand that their president was serious about this idea. While the expenditure was somewhat painful, it turned out to be the key; from that point forward, the employees knew that they could trust what the company said.

Also, we changed the company motto, which had been "Honor corporate results and honor people," to "Honor people and honor corporate results." We recommitted ourselves to being concerned for the individual.

Along with that, in fall of 1990 we started five-year plans on seven projects as part of the MR-21 campaign. This program was supposed to completely rework seven issues dealing with human resource systems, welfare systems, education, compensation systems, etc. Through this activity we were able to create a system which would draw the entire company together.

Q: Your firm had been already promoting TQC for a long time. How did that fit with PPORF?

Takaishi: Because we had been working on TQC for 20 years, we had created a solid base of small group improvement activities. We integrated these into the team activities that are part of the 20 Keys. Because of this, we scored high on the improvement team key from the start.

Q: And the secret of your success in implementing the 20 Keys?

Takaishi: In part it was the enthusiastic flag-waving of the people at the top. Because middle management support is critical, vector alignment took time. One significant point was assigning a "Key Leader" for each of the 20 Keys. We integrated the keys into people's jobs and proactively selected the people for the leadership roles.

Along with that, the PPORF office was indispensable. It was a group of specialists to communicate top management's plans accurately to the organization. They became a formal part of the organization.

Q: You appear to believe that it is critical for top management to take the reins; what specifically did you do?

Takaishi: I also had to do my homework—after all, we had been chosen as the model factory. We listened to the consultant who visited us each month. At first we thought we should raise weak points before the consultant had a chance to get to them, so we ended up criticizing individuals in front of everybody else.

While at first this was important in motivating people, after about 6 months it led to hard feelings, so we decided not to do it anymore.

When it came to selecting individual leaders, we took advice from the PPORF office, so the activities ran smoothly.

Q: Two years have passed since the implementation. Have you seen specific results yet?

Takaishi: By our numbers for the second half of 1992, total productivity was up 10 percent over the previous year. However, as I said, we are emphasizing respect for humanity over productivity. Because we want to make our company into one where our employees are glad that they have jobs here, we don't talk a lot in terms of productivity. The company that can build binding relationships with its employees is a powerful company.

Now that we have implemented the 20 Keys, everybody greets each other in the hallway, which is very different than before. I think the biggest result of this program is that people are able to talk to each other about many different things, making this a brighter place. In our recent companywide presentation meetings, one factory manager did speak on the theme of increasing productivity, but since the workplace has lightened up so much, it was okay.

Q: What are your plans for PPORF in the future?

Takaishi: Although we have not formally decided yet, ultimately we would like to go for the PPORF gold medal. We are working hard to become the top of our industry. When we say "top," what we are targeting is not just top quality, but also top in terms of cost, and faster than any other company on all fronts.

What we want to do is target the bronze medal in 1993, the silver medal in 1994, and then about four years out, the gold medal.

Because the quality of our people has progressed, you could say that, to some extent, we have already built the foundation.

Now policies I have held for some time—to always have an attitude which makes the workplace a lighter place, and to work on building people before we build things—are finally being realized through the 20 Keys.

Starting All 20 Keys Together to Strengthen Systems, Structures, and Cultures

by the PPORF Activity Office

Seiko Instruments Industries (SII) has catapulted forward under the watchwords "high technology with watches at the base." Morioka Seiko, an important affiliate to Seiko Instruments, accounts for approximately 90 percent of Seiko's domestic [Japanese] branded watch production (see Figures 1 and 2).

Figure 1: **Morioka Seiko and the Seiko Group**

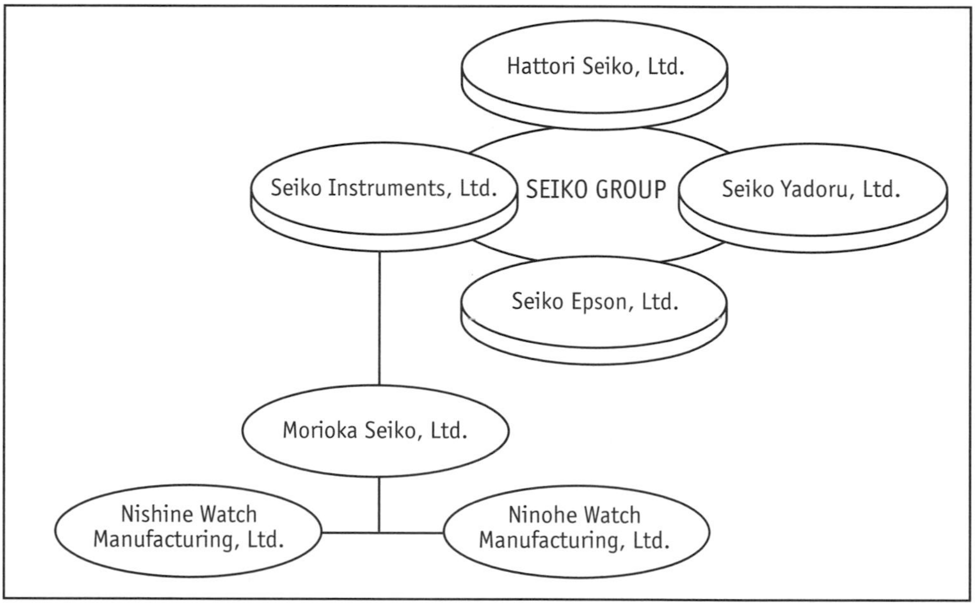

Morioka Seiko was originally started when a watch parts manufacturing factory was built as the Seiko Group was expanding its manufacturing scope, and thereafter it began manufacturing wrist watches.

Recently, as a factory automation (FA) factory, it has perfectly automated all of its processes from parts manufacturing to assembly to test to shipping, thereby establishing a system wherein the equipment can operate for longer hours and whereby the firm is able to respond to the diverse needs of the customers.

The corporate motto is "Respect for humanity, respect for results." We are also investing in benefits and programs for our employee, such as the preschool we opened on our premises in April, 1992.

Figure 2: **SII Watch Division PPORF Implementation Companies**

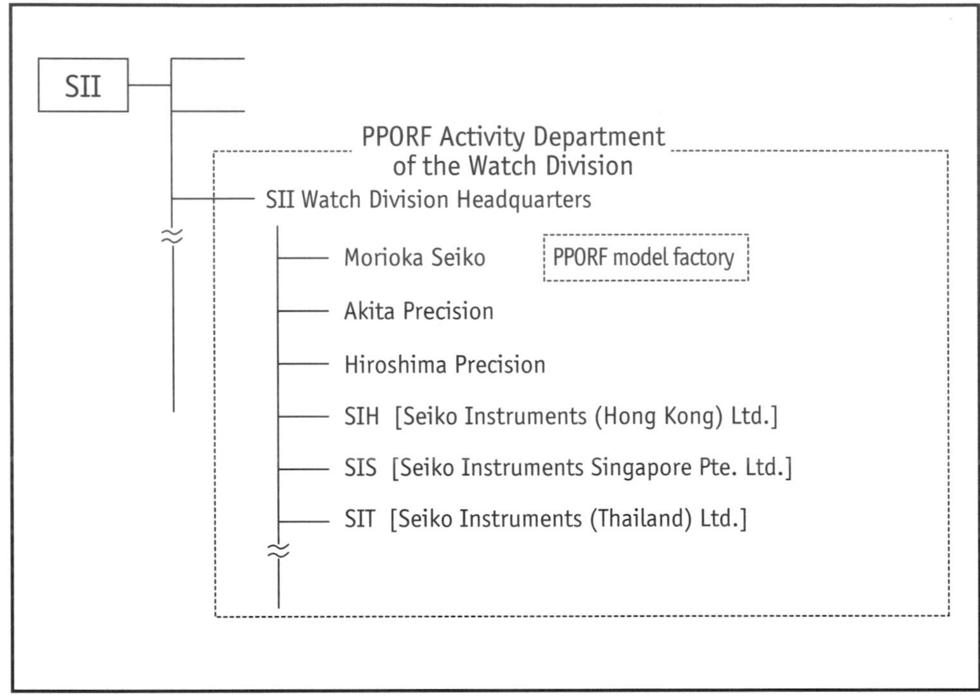

When the firm was first established, we manufactured screws, pins, and other parts for mechanical watches. After that, the assembly and inspection of mechanical watches was done by hand, and after wristwatches moved to quartz action, we did integrated manufacturing of inexpensive products. At this time two affiliate factories were established as wholly owned subsidiaries of Morioka Seiko.

The newest FA factory was built three years ago. Within this clean room environment an automation system was built for all processes, from parts manufacturing though assembly and test.

Based on the unification policies of the parent company, Seiko Instruments, the wristwatch manufacturing functions of the Keiyo Region were moved to the Tohoku Manufacturing Park. Our firm was positioned centrally to these operations.

The subject of this discussion is the Morioka Seiko PPORF Activities begun in February, 1991 under the direction of consultants from the PPORF Development Institute, activities implemented to improve the health of the manufacturing operations of the firm. A summary of these activities is presented on the following pages.

Activities to Strengthen Our Manufacturing Before PPORF Implementation

Under the direction of our parent company, Seiko Instruments, we have implemented many programs to strengthen our systems and structures since our firm was first established. These include:

- QC activities
- Small group activities
- Improvement suggestion activities
- NPS
- IE
- VE/VA
- Top management TQC/QC inspections

Our QC activities and improvement suggestion activities were quite active, and we had even presented at external meetings sponsored by the Union of Japanese Scientists and Engineers. However, many problems and issues still remained before the company could make the next real improvement. Moreover, each of these activities was done in isolation; no links were formed to unite all the workers, and there was some doubt that all employees actually participated. Although targets and plans were established, we were unable to instill strong enough conviction in the employees to move them to action. People understood the improvement programs on an intellectual level, but they were not stirred to participate. Upon reflection we wondered if this lack of excitement might not be traced to our reliance on logic and argument as our first approach.

Our Objectives (Medium-Term Hoshins)

The market for the wristwatches we manufacture was maturing, and the demand had already shifted from functional products to aesthetic products. There was no potential for any large increases in volume, and retail prices for our products were falling rapidly.

Under these circumstances, top management gave our factory the extremely challenging central role in making our industrial group the strongest industrial group in watches in the world. Although there were still many problems and issues to be resolved, the employees committed themselves completely to achieving this goal and thereby helping the firm grow (see Figure 3).

Figure 3: **Company Environment and PPORF**

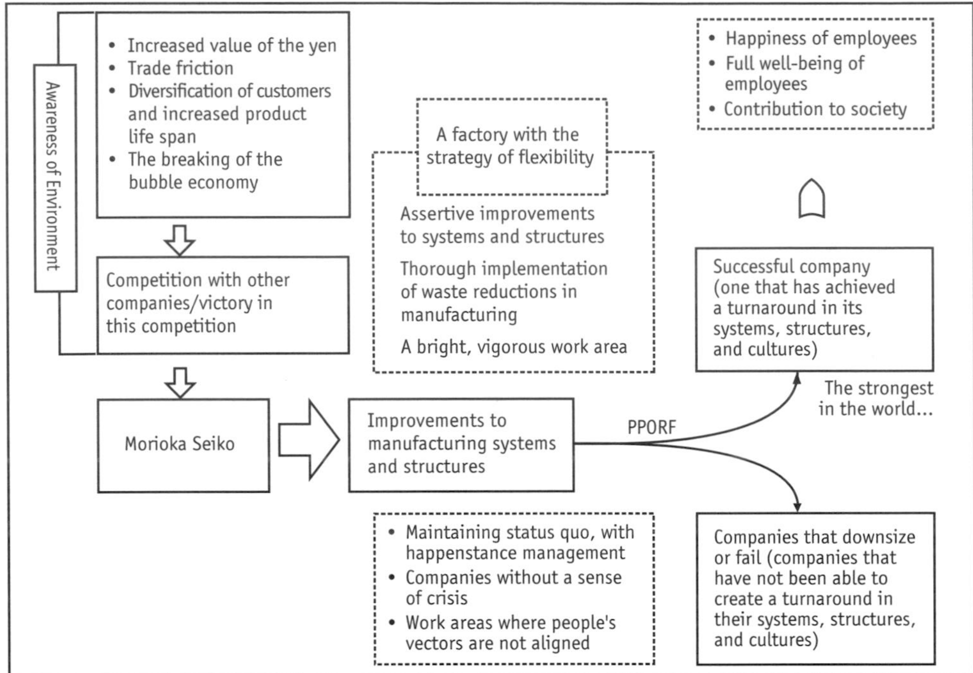

The Introduction of PPORF

At the Quality Control Conference of November, 1990, top management announced that the PPORF 20 Keys program would be implemented. The objectives were to:

1. Greatly increase the morale and levels of activity of each employee,
2. Double productivity, and
3. Offer customers throughout the world watches they find desirable and will readily purchase.

But how were we to make this a reality? What would be our methods, our "secret weapon"? Top management decided that the PPORF method would best fill these needs.

The PPORF Model Factory

After the top management proclamation we immediately started preparations for implementing PPORF. Although all watch business departments in Seiko Instruments started at work at the same time, our company was designated as the

Figure 4: **Fundamental Medium-Term Plan for WJ-PPORF**

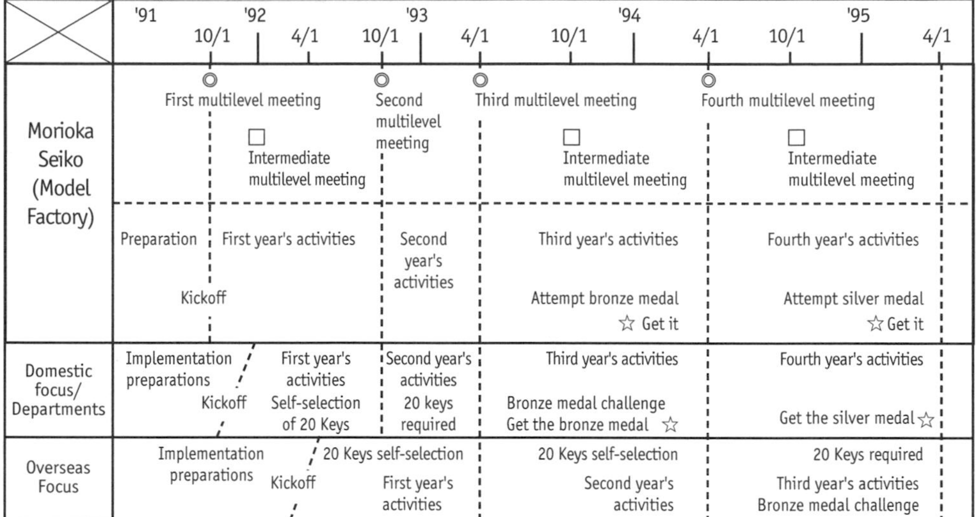

PPORF "Model Factory," and, beginning in February 1991, received direction directly from the PPORF Development Institute.

Although the word "model" sounds good, frankly, we thought something terrible had come upon us. However, we realized that we had become the "guinea pig" factory for PPORF, so we committed ourselves to thoroughly absorbing the 20 Keys methodology. True to the commitments we made, we held research and practice meetings twice a month, and even today we humbly study the direction received from our teachers as we accumulate experience and improvements (see Figure 4).

August was hot in the backroads town of Iwata. About 260 managers, supervisors, and factory leaders gathered together in the company gymnasium for the first multilevel meeting, under the direction of the company president (see Photograph 1). The president explained the companywide objectives and fundamental policies, and asked us to make and execute plans to achieve them.

To ensure that our efforts did not fail midcourse, this meeting also served as a point of departure from previous activities. Although this was a multilevel meeting, it did not include all employees. Those who did not attend received explanations through the formal work system, allowing all employees to "align their vectors" (see Key 2). To give all employees instruction and explanations from top management regarding PPORF, an all-employee PPORF meeting was held to ensure thorough participation in the activities.

Kickoff

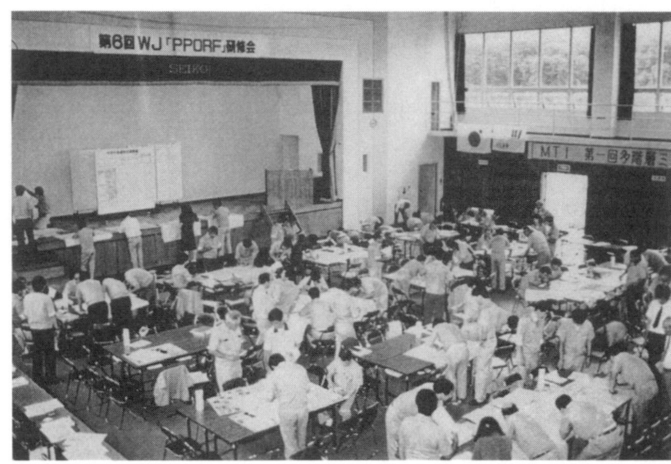

Photo 1: The first multilevel meeting

The PPORF activities were kicked off on October 1st. That morning was different from the opening day of any other program we had done before. Although everybody recognized that PPORF activities had to be based on strong commitment, we also wanted to promote the activities in a fun and happy way, so we used a handbill campaign.

The leaders designated for each of the 20 Keys of PPORF, along with all of the managers, wore Japanese-style headbands, raised battle flags, and awaited the arrival of the workers, handing each person a special kickoff handbill (see Photograph 2). This might sound silly, but it set this activity apart from all previous activities. We wanted everyone to feel like participating, so we tried to set an infectious spirit that would pull people in. We also served special refreshments to all the employees to make sure the activities started in a fun atmosphere.

Highlights of the Activities

1. Each work area (including the line and staff departments) addressed seriously the next step in each of the 20 Keys.

At first our master consultant, Mr. Kobayashi from the PPORF Development Institute, was worried. He asked, "Are you really prepared to work on all 20 keys at once? That will be terribly difficult!" With the enthusiasm and support of our president, we answered with an immediate "Yes!"

It's true, however, that things were rough around the time of the kickoff. On top of our normal workload we now had the additional burden of PPORF. Moreover, we had the kickoff without having had training in all 20 Keys, meaning that different managers and factory leaders would create their own individual action plans, requiring correction later by Mr. Kobayashi (see Photograph 3). He pointed out problems such as goals that were not described quantitatively, and improvement areas that were not clearly defined.

Photo 2: Managers distributing handbills on the morning of the kickoff

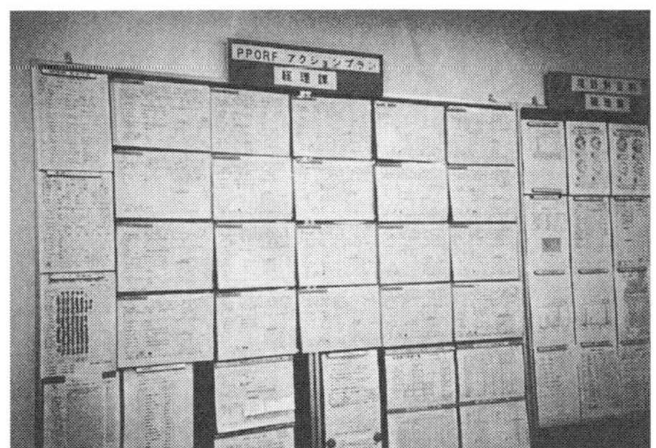

Photo 3: Action plans displayed to the work area after corrections and revisions

Managers above the leader level rechecked the company's fundamental hoshins and objectives, and we investigated again what each work area must do to reach those goals, determining the levels to which they must perform.

2. We began all activities with a model implementation, then deployed it horizontally.

The most important examples to promote activities are models that people can see with their own eyes. Following this philosophy, we created models on the work area-unit level, and deployed them horizontally.

These models included the 4S model work area, stores for consolidating work-in-process, and single changeover machines that had achieved internal changeovers in under 10 minutes. Even the staff had model desks that demonstrated how to improve efficiency at their work desks, and "single file" cabinets that allowed people to retrieve files in less than 1 minute. There were also areas where people painted the walls and the equipment on the work floor. (See Photographs 4 through 10 on the next page.)

When success was achieved in these advance areas, the company president reviewed the models and presented awards on the work floor in front of all the employees.

3. A research group was created to publicize examples of work floor improvements.

A PPORF research group was formed to serve as a venue for publicizing examples of shopfloor improvements. Mr. Kobayashi attended the research group and offered instruction (see Photograph 11), but the group also served as a forum where different work areas could meet to share the results of their activities.

The research group presented results of the cumulative improvements to large numbers of people (see Photograph 12). These activities were well received even by work areas that in the past had not gotten involved in activities.

Photo 4: Challenge boards were posted in the model areas

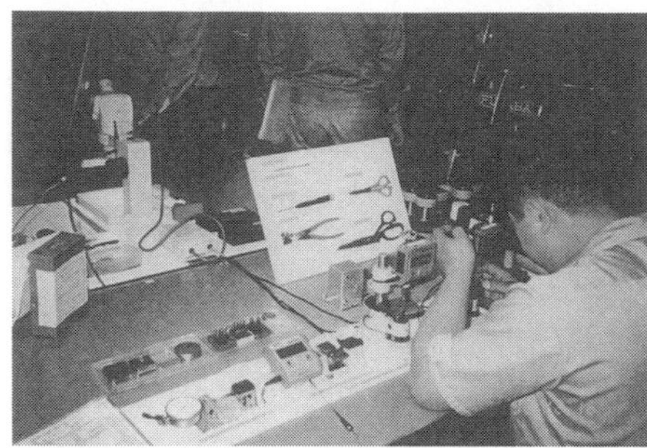

Photo 5: Tools were kept convenient on slantboards

Photo 6: The staff areas accepted the challenge of the "model desk"

Photo 7: "Single file" shelves

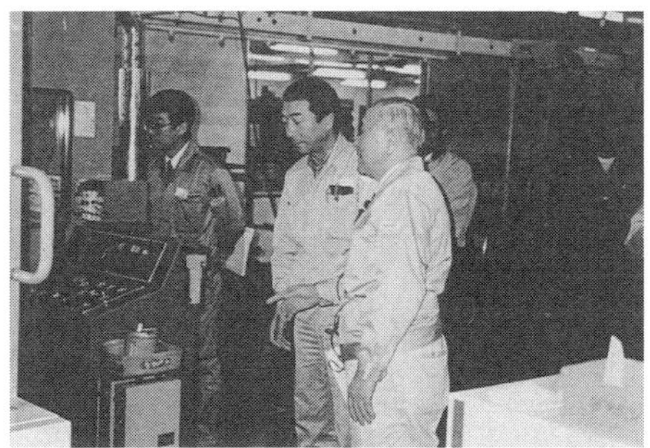

Photo 8: Mr. Kobayashi inspecting the plant floor

Photo 9: "Single file" shelves

Photo 10: Single changeover was also achieved in the clean assembly factory

Photo 11: The staff accepts the challenge of the "single file" (Banner: "Open to the Public: Single Changeover Underway")

The work group presenting its improvements interacted with the listeners, emphasizing questions and answers. This type of interaction played a major role in participatory study.

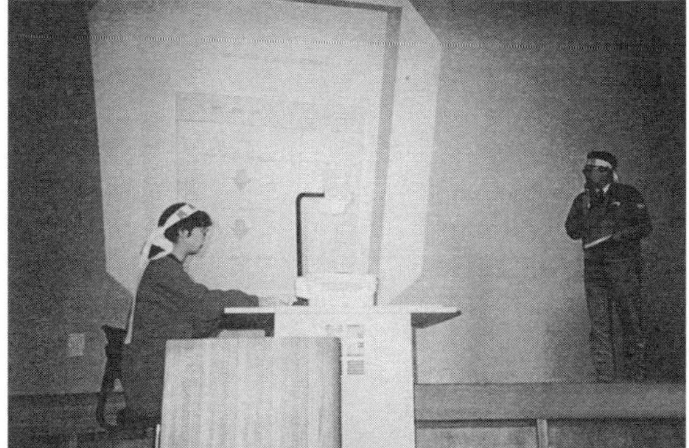

Photo 12: A group presents examples of its improvements

Attitudes and Keywords

"Key leaders" were established as companywide cross-sectional promotion experts for each of the 20 Keys of PPORF. The principles used by these leaders in promoting their individual keys included the following:

1. Open communication is the starting point for everything: the right word to use is the word that can be understood by everyone.
   - Speak frankly, but be kind and gentle.
   - Use appropriate words
   - Build an environment, an atmosphere, and a company way of doing things.
2. 5S is the starting point.
   - Pay attention to 4S (cleaning, organizing, maintaining cleanliness, organized cleanup) and time control. Don't forget to "4S" your own head as well!
3. Think big/act small: Success in big things is done by accumulating improvements.
   - Welcome small improvements.
   - Use natural competitions and make games of achieving goals.
4. Develop people and organizations that compete against themselves; empower these and they will each make progress.
5. Crises and opportunities are the same thing: A situation may be an opportunity or a crisis depending on how one addresses it and how one thinks about it.
   - Commitment and challenge
   - Time functions
6. Our competitors and our clients are the entire world: We too are taking on the world.

Results of Activities

The PPORF Evaluation Point Radar Chart

At the time of this writing, the first year's activities (October 1991 to September 1992) have been completed. Using PPORF maps, self-evaluations were performed on the work floor-unit level and then totaled (see Figure 5).

Figure 5: **PPORF Score Radar Chart**

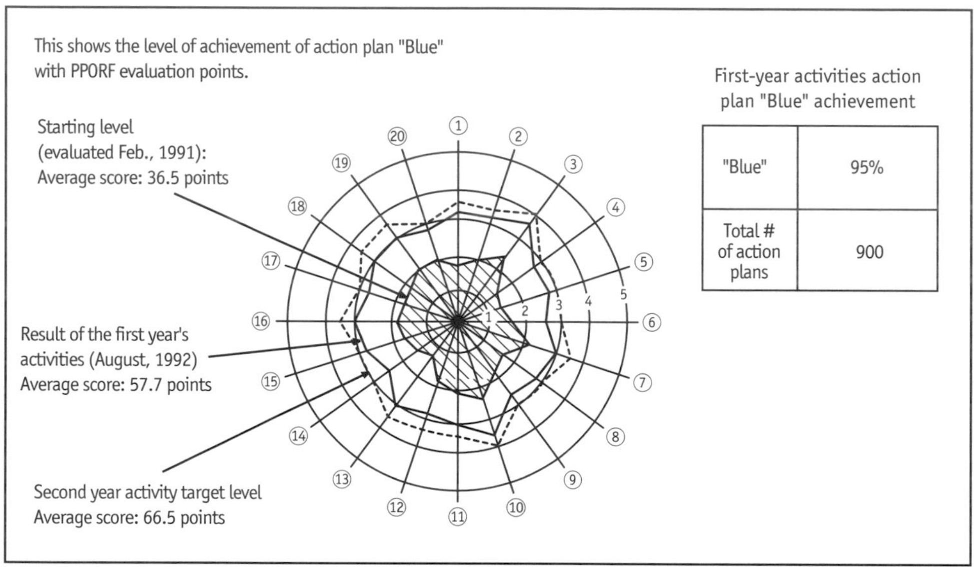

Action Plan Achievement

Five months after the kickoff in February 1992, we held a midterm multilevel meeting (see Photograph 13). At this midpoint in the activities we traced the results of the activity plans and checked the activity plans for the second half of the activities.

Photo 13: Second multilevel meeting (vector alignment for the second year's activities, and proclamation from the company president)

At that point, the results were on target in less than half of the cases. This was no different than previous activities, and it presented a sense of crisis which, at the suggestion of the factory manager (who was also the PPORF promotion headquarters manager) led to the creation of the "PPORF Come-up Council" for the section managers and the 20 Keys leaders. This meeting was held twice a month. Its objective was to check and track the details of each activity on a 1- or 2-month basis. Everyone got together to help the slow areas catch up, and in the August multilevel meeting or at least by the end of the activities in September, more than 90 percent of the plans had been successfully completed.

Promoting the Use of Microprocessors (Computers)

When compared to the use of microprocessors in the production equipment at that time, the use of microprocessors and computers in the staff departments was lagging. Because of this, we poured our efforts into using microprocessors (office automation equipment) in the staff departments as well, and made this the topic of our activities.

The focus of our activities for the first year was to eradicate computer "phobia" in the staff departments.

Computer Training

We first implemented computer education in order to achieve the first-year target of "assertively using automated equipment in improving our office work to expedite data processing and eliminate paper." Our teacher was one of the regular office workers who happened to like computers.

- Promotion of computer use within the department

Personal computers: Software training was given to 120 people, 4 sessions each.

Host computer: Training was given for Real Mapper, a database problem-solving application.

- Word processing training was provided to all managers of section manager class and above.

Because some managers lacked skill with word processors, the objective of this training was to enable them to draw up their own plans and documents by themselves. All managers achieved at least a rudimentary skill level.

- Data input accuracy was improved, contributing greatly to the creation of new production, POP, human resources, financial, and OCR systems.

Control Data and the Use of Microprocessors within the Factory

We established control items, standard levels (current levels), target levels, and critical action items so that all sections in all work areas within the factory could actually use the computers. One control item we adopted was to increase the number of computerized operations by 30 percent, and as a result of our first-year's activity using microprocessors we improved our operation time by 26.4 percent over the previous year.

By doing this, we effectively eradicated computer phobia. Computers are easy to use and play a role as tools to improve the effectiveness of work.

Summary

Less than two years have elapsed since we have implemented PPORF. In this time, all employees have experienced its excellent results, and the workplace has become a lighter and more dynamic place.

During this time we have had many visitors to our factory, with a total of about 3,000 people in a year's time, including people from overseas. These people have made numerous comments about our systems, including: "Wow, this factory is clean!" "It seems as though productivity is really improving," and "I was greeted so nicely—it made me feel really good."

This isn't to say that we clean our factory only when we are expecting visitors. We could invite people into the factory in its everyday state.

These external stimuli, knowing that we are always being looked at and that people are interested in what we are doing, has tied back into enhanced motivation for improvements.

As each individual has internalized specific improvement strategies and gone through a change of awareness through the 20 Keys program, he or she enjoys the results of the improvements that have been made.

We worked on all 20 Keys from the beginning, and the nonproduction staff participated as well. Success depends on whether the staff has a strong conviction that each key applies to them as well, and whether they have the wisdom to desire to improve the efficiency of their jobs.

At this point we are starting to understand the true synergistic effects between the activities of each of the 20 Keys, and to see the role these activities play in problem solving.

We have no doubt that PPORF is going to continue well beyond these activities. As of this writing, the second-year's activities are underway, and we are already looking forward to working hard to attain the objectives of the third year as well. We want to achieve the bronze medal and silver medal PPORF award levels, and then we are targeting the objective of being the most powerful watchmaking group in the world.

PPORF Promotion Headquarters Manager:
Ryohei Aida (director and manufacturing factory manager)

PPORF Activity Office Members:
M. Kawamura (quality assurance department manager)
G. Ichikawa (quality assurance department, PPORF promotion section manager)
K. Saito (quality assurance department, PPORF promotion section subsection manager)

Factory Turnaround Document: Deployment Focusing on the Use of Microcomputers

PPORF and the Promotion of CAD/CAM

CAD/CAM systems were introduced to our company in May, 1987. At that time, our CAD operation technology was inadequate, our data base was inadequate, and our design support software was inadequate. In fact, it was faster for us to use traditional drafting.

PPORF was kicked off in our company in October, 1991 when the CAD/CAM system was more complete and the use of drafters had, for the most part, been eliminated. At that time the speed and accuracy of drafters in design and drawing activities had become inadequate. However, to respond to the diversification of market needs we needed increased reliability in our design system. What could we do to improve beyond where we were—and how could we do it given our limited human resources?

Mr. Kobayashi of the PPORF Development Institute instructed us to reject the status quo as we worked to improve our operations. First we performed a "lifestyle analysis" (time study) to expose the core of our design work. The results showed that approximately 70 percent of our time was spent in activities related to the actual work, with the rest spent in telephone calls, searching for materials, and coordinating (in descending order). The actual work involved tasks such as investigations, research, thinking, making plans, making designs, making drawings, reviewing the drawings, and so forth. Even if we could improve on "waste" operations that do not contribute to the actual work, these improvements would not improve our efficiency to any great extent. We knew that we must improve the efficiency of the work itself. However, we continued to struggle because we did not know what we should improve nor how to do it.

We started the first work sampling study (Key 13) while we were thus engaged (see Figure 6). During this effort we ran into a problem involving the sampling check sheet used by both the direct departments and the indirect departments. This problem was that "thinking" in the design department was treated as a wasteful operation. In our first year of implementation, even the PPORF activity office began their critique of our operations with "there is a lack of standardization" that we should resolve by using standard operating procedures. However, the design department was not convinced; did that mean that they were not supposed to think? Did that mean that mutually examining one another's drawings was wasteful? Discussion of these and similar concerns became somewhat heated, and a fair amount of time passed before they developed some degree of understanding.

Figure 6: **Categories of Operations**

* Recorded as actual work

		Detail of Category	
Actual Work		Operating equipment, assembly, changeover—includes movement of less than 3 steps (approx.1.5 meters) Visual inspections, cleaning equipment Checking Control items (ledgers, progress), operating OA equipment, writing, calculating receiving products *Operating and PPORF improvements	
Monitoring	1	Thinking	
	2	Inspecting	① Observing equipment during operation
			② Inspecting equipment when it is not operating
Searching (retrieving)		Searching for jigs, tools, or materials (including data and forms) or retrieving something from storage.	
Transporting		Exceeding 3 steps, moving while carrying something	
Walking around		Exceeding 3 steps, moving without carrying something	
Talking	1	Telephone	
	2	Discussion	Meetings within the company, morning meetings, etc.
	3	Talking	Operator instructions, communications, consultation
Away from seat		Away from the work area	
Other		Cleaning, with visitors, resting, exercising	

On the first work sampling the design department scored only 46 percent actual work and 13 percent thinking/deriving ideas. This was incomparably bad when compared with other departments. If they rejected the status quo and attacked their "thinking time," what would happen?

The design department within our firm creates primarily jigs for assembly and inspection measurement tools. Although there is newly developed equipment on the unit level, it is actually rather rare; most of our design work is spent on designing things similar to what we have designed before. Because of this, we wondered whether it was possible to have "automatic" design. If the interactive CAD method could make it possible to automate the design process—making and outputting drawings by only inputting the data that we change—it would surely lead to wholesale improvements in efficiency.

Because of this, we started on a drawings standardization program targeting automatic design. We gained the cooperation of the programmers and worked hard to make it a reality.

Although the initial experiments took considerable time, we cleared the mountain of problems we encountered, and between June 1 and October 1 we developed the ability to design better and faster than we had in the past.

Of course, this improvement could not have succeeded without everyone's participation. Success flowed from PPORF's full participation and its integration of top-down and bottom-up methods.

When you consider Key 18, "Using Microprocessors," it is natural to include CAD/CAM in your thinking about ways to apply computers. Although ultimately computer operations are most critical in the direct production departments, the PPORF activities made us aware of the importance of the contributions of indirect departments, including the design department. This is based on the notion of respect for humanity; in the 20 Keys approach, the individual is the key.

Photo 14: PPORF promotes the use of CAD/CAM

Keeping in mind that the development and design departments are the source of much waste that can be eliminated, we strove to double productivity through promoting CAD/CAM in PPORF activities (see Photograph 14).

PPORF and the Promotion of POP

Implementation of a New Production Control System

The completion and deployment of the new assembly factory in 1989 was a major turning point for activities using microprocessors in our company.

Firmly positioned as the focus of watch manufacturing in Seiko Instruments, this plant not only implemented leading-edge assembly automation equipment, but also implemented automatic warehousing and totally automated transportation systems to improve material flow in new ways.

Along with these "hardware" improvements, we also were determined to implement a new production control system that used online real-time processing based on orders from the production plan, upgrading from the manual planning methods wherein results were processed in batches (see Figure 7). After researching the specifications and developing the software, we started out by running master control only and gradually adding the subsystems until, at present, all major systems are running.

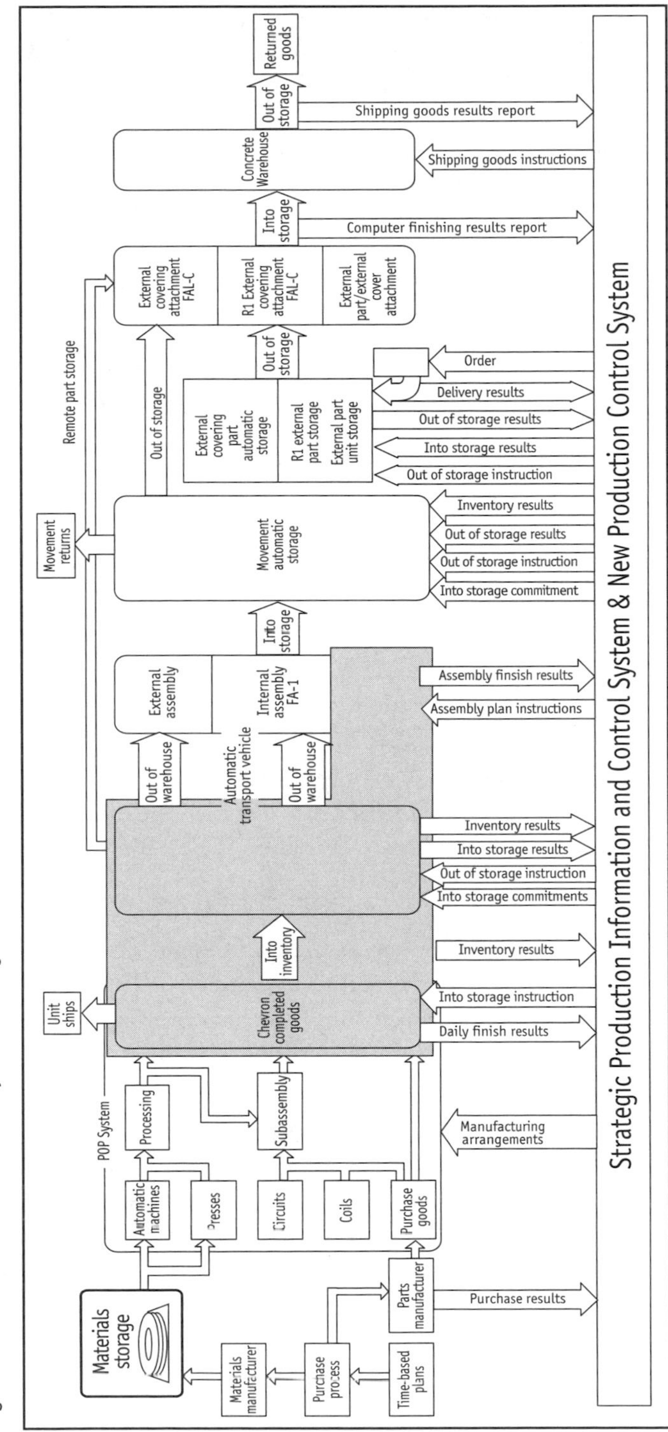

Figure 7: **Morioka Seiko new watch production system overview**

Photo 15: The subsystem assembly machine and the production control system

Photo 16: The software input/output was also done by the operators themselves

The features of this new production control system include the following:

- Production instructions based on the production plan
- Progress control based on an order number method
- Plan smoothing simulations in assembly
- End-user computing using a fourth-generation language (see Photographs 15 and 16)
- Easy input using bar codes
- Integrated master control
- Online real-time results accumulation
- Make-to-order production with virtually zero inventory

The production control system was implemented to control the processes from receiving to shipping after assembly, synchronized with the operation of the newly built factory.

The Decision to Implement the POP System and the First Attempt

On the other hand, when we looked at the manufacturing of parts, most of the management was done by hand, based on traditional-style ledgers. The movement toward high-variety small-lot manufacturing (due to the diversification of customer needs), combined with the increasing intensification of the manufacturing process, has pushed this manual control system to its limits.

Because of this, we were determined to implement a POP system (a point-of-production information control system) as a part of the new production control system. We asked Seiko Instruments to perform the development activities from the preliminary investigations to set the specifications, to the actual production of the program.

We entered the data transfer stage one year later, in April, 1991. The data from the ledgers was entered into the computer in parallel with the daily operations.

This made more work than originally anticipated because of the load involved with the inputting operations, the timing of the changeover, the work involved in checking the input data, and so on. The work that had been progressing so well when the system was being structured now ground to a halt.

We decided to implement PPORF while we were still in this situation of "one step forward and two steps back." During this time we began to see the big picture of 20 Keys activities in the pre-implementation training.

We initiated POP system explanation meetings and study meetings with the involved departments, and got the people who were actually in charge of using the system to become more aware of its necessity. To get them to understand the need for the system, we explained to them how the system would play a major role in working on several PPORF keys such as use of microprocessors, reducing inventory, and process control.

After that, all the data was entered within a year after operations were begun, an achievement owing to proactive efforts after work and on holidays under the cooperation and leadership of the involved department managers. This made possible the first stage of the POP system, that of being able to total the production results. The following effects were confirmed:

1. Paper reductions (reducing the ledgers and the control books)
2. Improved precision of the motion chart (the process chart)
3. Integration of a shared results database
4. Provision of warehousing information related to the assembly plan
5. Reduction of inputting errors
6. Reduction of total number of errors in monthly reports
7. Provision of control materials in a timely manner

Addressing the Planning System: Starting the Second Stage

Although the objectives of the POP system were to provide real-time day-to-day processing of data generated in the factory and to provide this information to the work floor managers and the people responsible for production control, once they began to understand how useful this information was, they began to demand planning data as well.

The parts manufacturing planning data was processed by a host computer in single-lot units of daily production instructions, and distributed into each work area in ledgers known as "arrangement books." On the work floor the control method was to use color overlays to show the progress; however, because the number of parts was increasing daily, it was impossible to control all parts in this way.

In this situation we upgraded the functions of the system so that as soon as the host computer arrangement data was input into the POP system, the results data which had been input could be accessed and variances from the daily arrangements (slow lots or fast lots) could be viewed in color. This enhancement was released in October, 1991.

The System Structure

Ethernet was selected for the network. We selected a 10BASE5 cable because of its robustness to noise.

When the system was first functioning, we had only a single strand of network cable. We now have three cables running through the ceilings in the factory building to serve an increased number of shopfloor terminals, a new factory annex added in January, 1992, and terminals in conference rooms.

Also, because the amount of data handled in the planning system is so great, we now have online data exchange. This is the first time our company has had connections between different types of machines. The program was developed using the C language, and database software is not used (see Figure 8).

Figure 8: **Network by connecting different types of equipment**

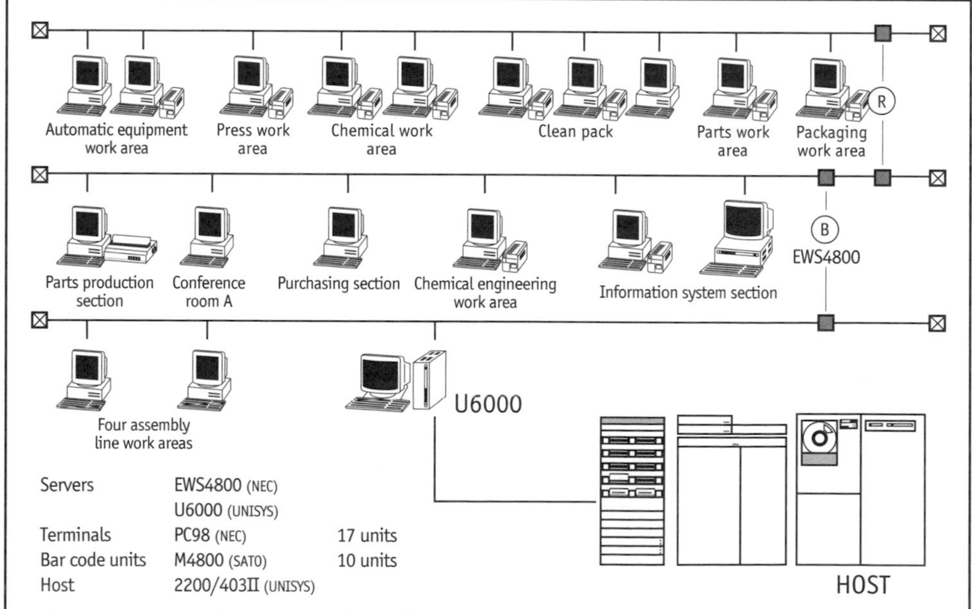

Improvements to Equipment Built In-House (Equipment Developed by the Company)

Below we present autonomous improvements made through the 20 Keys to equipment built in-house.

The Production Control System

The production control system using FA computers is a representative example of use of computers in PPORF.

This is a real-time system that links the subassembly machines and coil manufacturing line to FA computers used by the manufacturing department to automatically collect data on units produced, equipment stops and their reasons, number of defects, number of defects per cause, cycle time, and other information. The system automatically tabulates the information, immediately showing the causes for reductions in uptime and through-production ratios.

This system makes possible long-term stable operations and increased uptime and through-production ratios of the line, based on actions that can be taken immediately after reviewing the data collected.

This data is stored on the hard disk for a specified period of time, and can be printed out in the form of daily reports, monthly reports, and other ledgers, or in graphical forms as necessary. The system greatly reduces the amount of work by individuals in tabulating this information.

The next focus is horizontal deployment of this system and creation of an integrated system that includes the control of production flow by networking with higher-level computers.

Reducing the Equipment Adjustment Time on Automated Assembly Lines

The improvement to the unit adjustment method in the movement assembly line is an example of an improvement to reduce changeover time.

Automated assembly lines normally run at full uptime so they cannot be stopped during the day. Because of the high use ratios, it is necessary to minimize line-stop loss by performing major changeovers on holidays or late at night. However, even when changeovers are done at these off hours, there is still a limited amount of time available; it is extremely difficult to complete the changeover according to plan.

As a result there are now several revolving units prepared in advance, combining the units, the automatic feed equipment, and the controllers in a single set.

Thorough unit adjustment checks are performed in advance and changeovers are done by the set. This has greatly reduced the changeover time required in the line.

The team-based improvements included activities such as:

Photo 17: The IP gas line connectors have been converted to a one-touch system

- preparing revolving units
- "one-touch" conversion of valves and vacuum pipes (see Photo 17)
- using input/output board connectors
- standardization of attachment valves and types of centers.

The cumulative result of various innovations is that sets can be switched quickly and easily. The improvements were executed with relative ease because the assembly line in this company uses a system where each unit has its own controller (microcomputer).

Also, all checks including operating checks can be done completely offline because input into the controllers is done using personal computers during the preparation stage. Therefore online adjustments involve nothing more than a final check and can be done extremely quickly.

Implementing Single Changeover on the Automatic Lathe

The automatic lathe is an automated machine developed in-house for secondary machining of watch components. Because each lathing machine was specialized for each individual watch part, single changeover (under 10 minutes) did not seem possible.

However, in the first year of PPORF implementation this equipment became the subject of single-changeover activities, and excellent single changeover was accomplished as the result of cumulative employee team improvements on the work floor. Main improvements included the following:

- standardization of methods and heights of automatic feed equipment (see Photograph 18)
- conversion of jigs to a one-touch method that indicates whether or not work is present
- revision of the collet chuck method from a pull system to a push system (see Photograph 19)
- conversion of air supply connectors (mini-couplers) to a one-touch system and simplification of air line identification by color-coding
- standardization of sequencer programs.

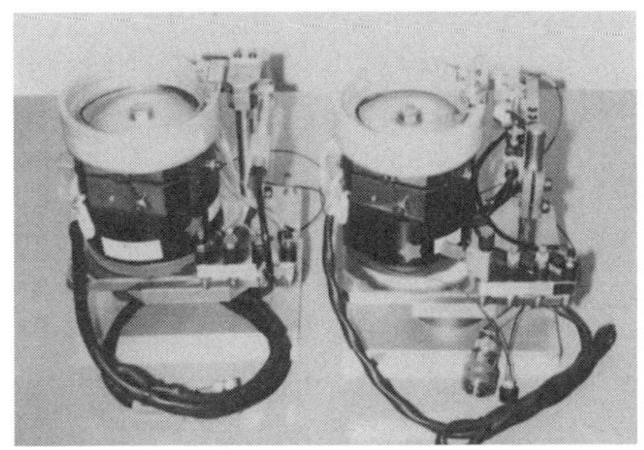

Photo 18: The automatic feed equipment adjusts to standardize the height if the parts are different

Photo 19: The improvement to the collet chuck

Single changeover was made possible by these improvements and by the cumulative effect of many smaller improvements.

We achieved single changeover on only a single unit in the first year after implementation, but in the second year this approach is being deployed horizontally to all units, and improvement team activities to achieve single changeovers are currently in progress.

An Automatic Instruction System for Changing Over Assembly Parts

The examples presented below show a system for supporting product flow when supplying structural components for watch movements on an assembly line. It describes the "assembly operator shopping" support system (the line input part changeover instruction system) created for the new supply system that began in August, 1992 , in which the line operator goes to a parts shelf (called the "store" in PPORF) to "purchase" the parts needed for assembly (see Photograph 20).

In the past, kits were formed in which 20 to 25 parts of each movement were counted and packaged together and then stored on carts. This improvement activity sought to reduce the number of counting and packaging operations.

Figure 7 (page 255) showed the overall product flow in the factory today; the shaded regions show the relationships between parts storage (automatic storage) and the production line.

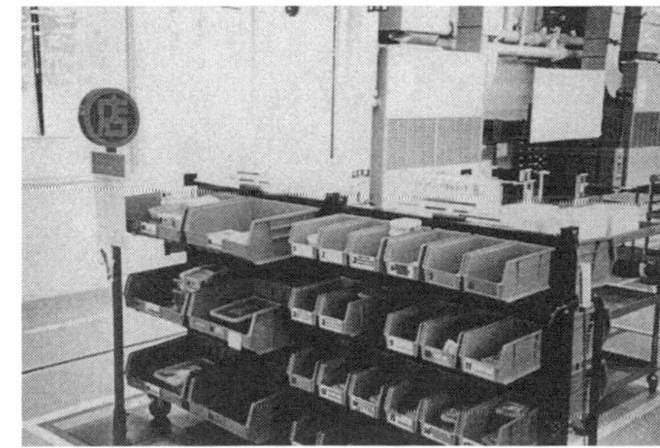

Photo 20: Following the changeover instruction document, parts are transferred to the panel racks (the store)

First, the parts for assembly are stored in the automatic warehouse in their manufacturing lot or purchased lot unit packages. The POP system bar code reader reports to the host computer that the lot has entered the automatic warehouse. Based on this, the host computer issues instructions to the automatic storage unit to retrieve from inventory those parts required by the assembly schedule (based on standard yields), and the automatic storage unit control computer automatically sends the required parts to each of the four assembly lines.

The parts used in assembly are supplied in manufacturing lot or purchased lot unit part counts, and the system is such that the automatic storage unit controls the surplus transfer (shown as "ST leftover" in Figure 7) so that it is always less than the lot packaging unit.

This system eliminates the need for assembly kits and packaging operations, and expedites the supply of replacement parts if there are accidental assembly errors. On the other hand, this material flow method adds annoying decision tasks such as the assembly operator having to select the parts required for assembly and "purchase" them from the "store," having to check whether leftover parts can be used in the next plan to be released, and then having to continually run the parts back.

To give a bit more detail, the four assembly lines are high-variety, low-volume lines, running 140 different types of movements on each line. When the operator has to decide whether the parts on hand can be used in the next assembly (i.e., whether they are shared parts or specialized parts), it can be a fairly risky judgment.

Because of this, before moving to the new system shown in Figure 7, we prepared an automatic production/printing system for a personal computer as in the "release part changeover instruction document" shown in Figure 9. Each day the line leaders would prepare a release part changeover instruction document for the following day's production schedule and post it in the "store." Photograph 20 shows the store and the release part changeover instruction document.

A summary description of the release part changeover instruction document automatic generation system follows.

System Overview

1. The system shown in Figure 8 is a supplementary system that operates on standard equipment (PC98) within the company. Thus its operations are simple and it can be used by assembly line personnel.

2. Program development and improvements were simple. Storing the master is simple as well.

3. When the product codes for the movement currently being assembled are input with the codes for the next movement to be assembled, using an interactive method, the following information automatically prints out:

- a list of the parts that can be recovered when the line is changed over, and the shelves where they are stored (i.e., the "store").

Figure 9: **Example of release part changeover instruction document**

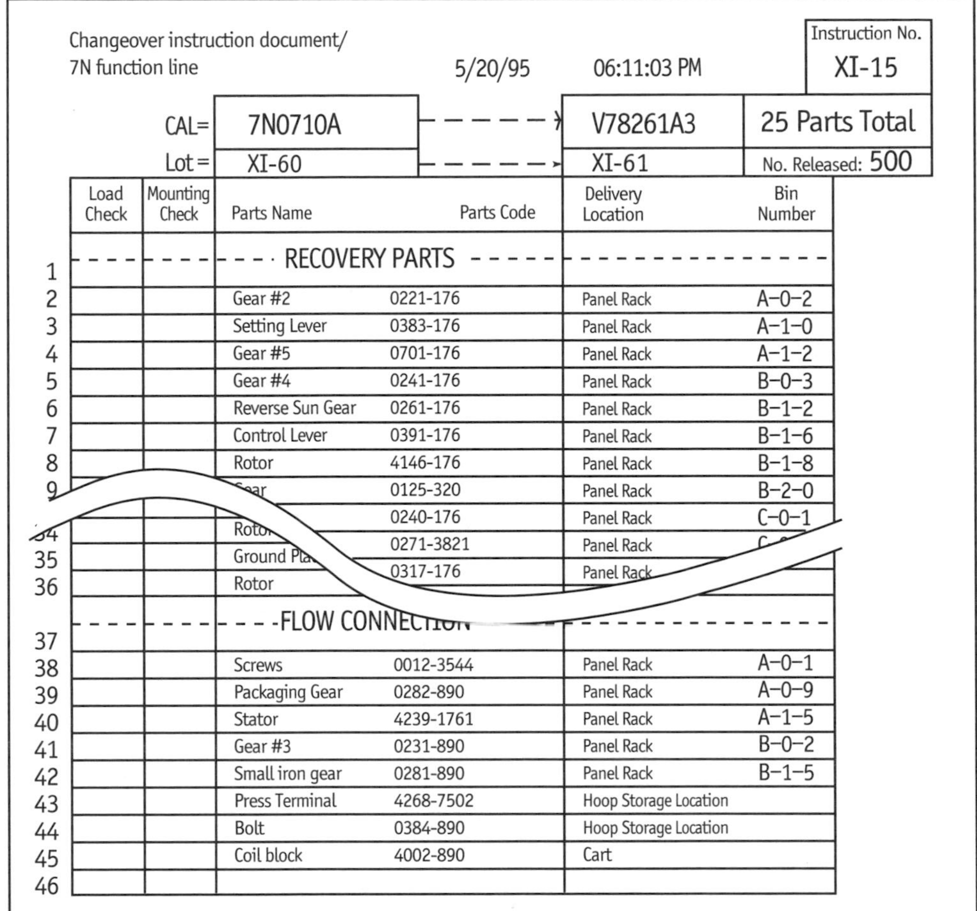

Changeover instruction document/
7N function line 5/20/95 06:11:03 PM

Instruction No. XI-15

CAL= 7N0710A → V78261A3 — 25 Parts Total

Lot= XI-60 → XI-61 — No. Released: 500

	Load Check	Mounting Check	Parts Name	Parts Code	Delivery Location	Bin Number
1			RECOVERY PARTS			
2			Gear #2	0221-176	Panel Rack	A-0-2
3			Setting Lever	0383-176	Panel Rack	A-1-0
4			Gear #5	0701-176	Panel Rack	A-1-2
5			Gear #4	0241-176	Panel Rack	B-0-3
6			Reverse Sun Gear	0261-176	Panel Rack	B-1-2
7			Control Lever	0391-176	Panel Rack	B-1-6
8			Rotor	4146-176	Panel Rack	B-1-8
9			...ar	0125-320	Panel Rack	B-2-0
				0240-176	Panel Rack	C-0-1
34			Roto...	0271-3821	Panel Rack	C-...
35			Ground Pla...	0317-176	Panel Rac...	
36			Rotor			
37			FLOW CONNE...			
38			Screws	0012-3544	Panel Rack	A-0-1
39			Packaging Gear	0282-890	Panel Rack	A-0-9
40			Stator	4239-1761	Panel Rack	A-1-5
41			Gear #3	0231-890	Panel Rack	B-0-2
42			Small iron gear	0281-890	Panel Rack	B-1-5
43			Press Terminal	4268-7502	Hoop Storage Location	
44			Bolt	0384-890	Hoop Storage Location	
45			Coil block	4002-890	Cart	
46						

- a list of common parts that will continue to be used in the next movement, along with their storage bin numbers.
- the total number of parts used in the next movement.
- the instruction date.

4. The instruction document number, the movement lot number, and the number to be fitted are input interactively, and the instruction document is printed.

5. The masters for the structural parts used in the movement can be maintained in real time, so when there are parts which have not been entered or when there are redundant entries, the errors can be taken care of.

Software Used

- Lotus 1-2-3 (a spreadsheet software package) with macro commands.

Output Format (see Figure 9)

Processing Time

- It takes about two minutes to print one form shown in Figure 9.

Effects

1. Simplified standard operations for the release of parts, leading to a reduced risk of erroneous production due to decreased parts release and specification mistakes.

2. The horizontal deployment of this and other programs and masters to other areas within the firm.

Topics and Improvements for the Future

1. Conversion of parts mastering and maintenance tasks to autonomous work. If possible, we would like to develop within the users the ability to restructure the programs (for example to extend the system to one which simultaneously issues unit machine changeover instructions).

2.The creation of a PC-based system for calculating inventory levels in the store. (In the materials flow method of Figure 7, this system would subtract the final part counts [i.e., the counts sold] from the actual inventory at the store by performing parts deployment, and also calculate the defect rates over time, along with other miscellaneous operations).

In the past, the term "programming" denoted a specialized industry performed by experts locked away in a computer room somewhere. As databases become more advanced, we have entered the age where users themselves have the opportunity for creative innovation.

Moreover, this creative innovation is expedited by the PPORF Keys focusing on using computers, empowering workers, and leading technology/site technology. Since May, 1992 we have been providing a Lotus 1-2-3 training session for new computer users so that we can continue our enhancement activities on the work floor and within the company in the future.

Because improvement of productivity in office work is so important, we must deal with this assignment carefully, with a "beginner's mind."

Appendix D

Case Study: Windfall Products, Inc.

by Eric Wolfe, vice president of Windfall Products, Inc.

Windfall Products was founded in 1976 as a producer of powder metal parts. Powder metal is a process in which iron powders are compacted with a press to form a part or other object. The part is then hardened in a furnace at almost 2100° Fahrenheit. The largest market is automotive, representing almost 75 percent of all powder metal parts produced. Other markets supplied include lawn and garden equipment, computers, business machines, and appliances.

Our company, located in St. Marys, Pennsylvania, has grown at an annual rate of over 30 percent to become the fourth largest producer of powder metal parts in the United States. That growth has been fueled by the increased use of powder metal in automotive parts. Before 1982, we survived by going after business from our competitors. Since that time, we have increased our business by developing new applications for powder metal. Today we are the world leader in soft magnetic powder metal parts. Even through the recessions of the '80s and '90s, we have been able to increase our business.

But something was missing. By the mid '80s the auto industry was in serious trouble with competition from Japan. They turned to their suppliers for help and for the first time we saw a crack in the armor. We had been running away from our inefficiencies. Our growth had outpaced problems in our operations, and by 1988, with major expansions coming in the near future, we began to question how well prepared we were. It was at this point we discovered what was missing. While sales and engineering were moving forward, the rest of the operation needed a vision—something more than "make tomorrow look more like today." We needed to make our operations a competitive tool to help our customers.

We knew we needed to change, but we weren't sure what we needed to do or become. We had heard of this thing called just-in-time manufacturing, so we started to read, visit as many companies as we could, and attend conferences. Two sources of information stood out: the American Production Inventory Control Society (APICS) and Productivity, Inc. Through all of this, one clear picture began to emerge—we needed to reduce our lot sizes and increase our flow of product.

We started with a project to clean the factory. What a success! Finally there was a place for everything and everything in its place.

Next, we started reducing setup times. Our molding presses typically took 6 to 8 hours to change over. Our first pilot project resulted in reducing changeover time to 30 minutes in less than 3 months. Total cost of materials for this project was less than $600. The employees involved were people who worked on the equipment, not engineers. The focus was on process—no gadgets, no gimmicks, just everyone doing it right.

To test their methods, the group asked someone who never set up a machine before to try to follow their methods. He set up the machine and had it running good parts in 42 minutes.

This group continued to reduce the changeover time to less than 10 minutes using Shigeo Shingo's SMED system. Another press was redesigned to be set up regularly in less than 3 minutes.

With results like this from our pilot we were very excited about our future prospects. With the pilot we had reduced the number of molding processes needed from 4 to 2, increased the efficiency by 30 percent, and almost eliminated tool breakage due to setup, all by reducing changeover time and lot sizes.

But another problem popped up. Customer service still wasn't any better. What happened? We did everything we were supposed to do. Except for one thing, and a walk to the shop floor said it loud and clear. We had improved everything but the bottleneck operation. This pointed to another problem. Our departmentalized structure had to go and we needed to give our company an understanding of managing the flow of product through a process.

We first went to work on how we were structured. Changing from a departmentalized process focus to a product focus was no easy task. It took months of planning meetings with every employee in the company on all three shifts before we made the change.

During the planning stages several significant points were outlined. The product focus organization, or Focused Factory, as we call it, would seek to create an environment for continuous improvement. Those people involved in the manufacturing process should be involved in its improvement. The manufacturing process would be organized into product focused teams identified by the technology required to manufacture the products. Team members would be involved in operations throughout the process, not just one department. The teams should evolve into self-sufficient subplants.

One very important question was left to be answered. What will the teams do? We still needed to be able to give our people to have a vision of what a perfect world would look like. Then along came the book *20 Keys to Workplace Improvement.* And with it came the very first time I had seen a simple way of educating people on what we needed to do to be a world class company. This, we thought, was the missing link. We had great people and now they had a direction to go. With support from Productivity, Inc. consultant Charles Skinner, we examined Kobayashi's 20 Keys system, adopted much of it, and changed some of it to meet our needs. This became our Keys to Continuous Improvement.

The following sections look at Windfall's Focused Factory, the Continuous Improvement keys, and some of the results we've attained with this approach.

What Is the Focused Factory?

The focused factory represents a fundamental rethinking of Windfall Products' approach to manufacturing. Our aim is to create a better environment for continuous improvement through employee ownership of the manufacturing process.

Previously, Windfall had a traditional departmental structure. Work was divided between those who produced and those who solved problems in that process. Such a division of labor assumes that the first group is not capable of the work performed by the second group. The Focused Factory declares this an erroneous assumption. The people involved in the manufacturing process are the people best suited to solve their own problems, if given responsibility for them and the opportunity to take action.

As a focused factory, Windfall Products is organized not by departments, but by teams. Teams were formed according to the technologies required to produce types of parts—magnetics, density-critical parts, and so forth. Team members will not simply perform one operation without knowledge or responsibility of the rest of the process. Jobs are being redefined to encourage learning of the entire process. The goal is to develop people who are experts not just in a single function, but in producing an entire group of parts. As team members develop this expertise, they will be better able to make improvements according to the Continuous Improvement Keys.

At present, we are extending the focused factory only to our direct manufacturing areas. However, teams will gradually assume the responsibilities of our manufacturing support departments, such as engineering and scheduling. These departments will not be eliminated, but instead freed up to develop greater expertise in their respective fields, passing newfound knowledge along to the teams. Ultimately, teams will evolve into self-sufficient "subplants."

Of course, for our team members to truly understand the products they make, they must understand their customers. We are greatly expanding customer contact, so everyone will be aware of our customers' problems and needs. We are confident that when our experts work directly with our customers, we can transform the customer-supplier relationship into a genuine partnership.

Continuous Improvement Keys at Windfall Products

The Continuous Improvement Keys are Windfall Products' definition of excellence in synchronous manufacturing. They represent our vision of the world class manufacturer we must become if we are to compete in a global marketplace.

Excellence in manufacturing is never achieved at a single stroke. It is the sum of sustained, critical examination of every step in the process, every piece of equipment, and every activity of every person involved. And it demands that the knowledge and insight of all experts be brought to bear on its attainment. Achieving excellence, in short, requires continuous improvement.

As we ascend through the levels of each key, the changes we effect will become more and more visible to all who visit and work here. Our progress will serve as clear testament to the vital, progressive spirit which has always distinguished the people of Windfall Products.

The following section outlines the criteria and levels of our keys, along with some comments about our implementation and results so far.

Key 1 - Manage Objectives

To effectively reach team goals, management and employees must determine objectives cooperatively, with everyone sharing ownership.

Level 1

- "Chain gang" style leadership—no clear management except for a boss at the top.

Level 2

- "Safety first" style leadership—the organization is better defined, with some direction from the top, but no one is sure what the direction means (example: slogans like "Safety First").

Level 3

- Clear instructions are communicated to team members.
- All objectives are measurable.
- All teams put their goals on charts and track progress.

Level 4

- The company develops shared objectives.
- The company develops shared strategies to meet those objectives.

Level 5

- There is a complete and measurable objective system.

A major project came out of our work here. We sorely lacked performance information for the shop floor. In fact, we had very little integrated information anywhere in our operation. Since 1991, we have been designing and implementing an information system to integrate our entire operation, as well as communicate with suppliers and customers. This has resulted in an incredible awareness of customer needs, costs, workloads, scrap rates, machine efficiencies, or any operational issue by everyone in our organization. I am impressed with how many people have gone on to learn how to use tools like Lotus 1-2-3 to create their own spreadsheets and learn to measure their team's performance.

Key 2 - Empower People to Make Improvement

For workplace improvements to be lasting, they must not only be executed in the workplace, but originate in the workplace. Many companies encourage employees to develop improvement ideas, but the best also allow people the freedom to execute those ideas. These improvements are displayed at each team's Information Center.

Level 1

- The company fosters team ideas, but uses other groups or other companies to build or modify equipment reflecting their ideas.

Level 2

- The company has installed—and uses—a plantwide Information Center.

Level 3

- Each team has and uses an Information Center.

Level 4

- The team can build its own low-cost automation or improvement devices.

Level 5

- Teams can design, build and implement their own improvements or automation devices.

Key 3 - Conduct Group Activities

Through group activities, the team learns to effectively manage itself to achieve greater productivity and efficiency. Group activities empower individuals to fully contribute their knowledge and experience toward the team's success.

Level 1

- No desire to start activities.

Level 2

- The company demonstrates an interest in group activities.
- Continuous improvement suggestions are encouraged.

Level 3

- Group activities have begun, but are not dynamic programs for improvement.

Level 4

- Group activities are enthusiastic and active.
- Group activities monitor performance in relation to established goals and objectives.

Level 5

- Goals and objectives are met by the group.

Many companies talk about empowerment but few that I have seen have taken it to the point we have. We have 650 people working in our company in approximately 130,000 square feet. On any day at any time you will find small groups of people working together on projects that they report on quarterly to their team members. Everything we do is based on involving people to drive change, not driving people to change.

Involvement also raises an enormous need for information and education. Education on how to solve problems, conduct meetings, or perform value analysis is very important for people put into a position to improve things. To support this we have two people who are full-time Continuous Improvement (CI) facilitators.

Their job is to help educate people in methods of continuous improvement and to conduct special workshops to help other people become facilitators.

The second and most important element of education is people relating to people. Without strong relationships among our people, "continuous" improvement can never happen. We have made quite a commitment to this through the Dale Carnegie program. Over 30 percent of our 650 people have gone through the program, and we are committed to providing every one of our people with the opportunity to go through this training. The course is based on developing positive relationships, building self-confidence, self-esteem, leadership skill, dealing with stress and worry, and developing enthusiasm in your life. The 12-week course is only a start. We also have a Dale Carnegie instructor on staff who conducts follow-up classes and works with people one-on-one to help them use the principles they have learned. This process of working with the whole person and not just the person at work is vital to our success and represents the primary focus of our Continuous Improvement program. If our people can continuously improve themselves, their families, and their communities, then Windfall Products will continuously improve also.

Key 4 - Clean and Organize

Before you can set priorities and plan the direction you want to take, you must clean and organize the plant. Cleaning and organizing are the most fundamental quality and productivity improvement activities.

Level 1

- Cigarette butts, scraps of paper, and tools are scattered around.

Level 2

- Clutter and piles of dirt lie against the walls.
- Passageways are not cleared.
- Unused items lean against the walls or pillars.
- Unused tools or equipment lie around.

Level 3

- Walkways are clear and the factory is clean, but storage areas are disorganized.
- Cabinets are locked and contents mixed together.

Level 4

- Machinery and equipment are clean.
- Storage areas are clearly distinguished, and show parallel lines and right angles. Cabinets should be unlocked.

Level 5

- Everyone cleans regularly from wall to wall.
- The work area is immaculate and tools are laid out squarely.

At the core of any successful organization is attitude. The easiest way to communicate attitude is sometimes without words. A clean, well-organized operation says more about quality than words can ever express. Our industry uses fines powders that are black and dirty; many companies could be mistaken for coal mines rather than manufacturing companies. We have set very high expectations of what "clean and organized" should be. This remains a challenge. Our theme is "a place for everything and everything in its place."

Key 5 - Develop Coupled Manufacturing

Coupled manufacturing links upstream and downstream processes such that a person receives inventory from a designated area or "coupling point," as though shopping in a store. All operations understand that the next operation is the customer. An operation notifies those before it when it needs partially completed inventory. This is also called a "Pull System."

Level 1

- Each operation functions independently of those before or after it.

Level 2

- All employees thoroughly understand the customer-supplier relationship as it applies to the company, the importance of coupling, and methods of achieving it.

Level 3

- The teams begin to identify and manage coupling points.

Level 4

- Coupling points are established throughout the manufacturing process.
- Teams begin to combine multiple products into common coupling points.

Level 5

- Many coupling points have been eliminated.
- The system is highly responsive to customer demand.

Again, education has been the key. Educating team leaders and team members. Evolving coupling points to cells has been a challenge for our engineers. They have been able to modify very large pieces of equipment so that that they can be moved. We have worked to eliminate monuments that force you to accept inefficiencies. All of this has resulted in an increase of product flow. As a result, our inventory turns are over 30 compared to our industry average of 9.

Key 6 - Improve Quality Assurance System

A true quality assurance system addresses many manufacturing challenges, such as reducing equipment failure, improving tool change methods, and mobilizing people as teams. As these challenges are met and overcome, the company is transformed from one where quality is ensured by sorting bad parts.

Level 1

- Quality assurance is the responsibility of the testers and inspectors.

Level 2

- All employees inspect for defects originating from their operation.

Level 3

- Statistics are taken to identify defective material. Defects and process variability are determined by statistical sampling.
- Effective corrective action meetings are held.

Level 4

- All teams understand and are implementing the basics of *poka-yoke* (mistake-proofing).

Level 5

- Poka-yoke and defect prevention systems are active throughout the plant.
- The in-process abnormality rate (scrap, rework) is less than .1 percent.
- Zero defects reach the customer.

Improving quality is our greatest challenge. Everything works to improve quality, but in today's world of measuring defects in parts per million, even one defect is too many. This is probably where Vaughn Beals from Harley-Davidson said, "Continuous improvement is continuous frustration." This is where everything is measured. Our poka-yoke devices and better procedures have reduced our defects by two-thirds. It's a lot to be proud of, but there's a long way to go.

Key 7 - Maintain Machines and Equipment

Preserving and maintaining the reliability of equipment is an essential task in a successful company. Maintenance and equipment experts are needed to develop a program of maintenance control. People who operate equipment are in the best position to monitor the day-to-day condition using checklists provided by these experts. The person using the equipment is the one responsible for keeping it running at maximum efficiency.

Level 1

- Run machines into the ground.

Level 2

- Perform preventive maintenance on most essential equipment.

Level 3

- Operators and setup people are aware that it is their responsibility to keep equipment from breaking down.
- Preventive maintenance occurs on all machines through operator support and checklists.
- Activities exist to eliminate losses from:

  a. Breakdowns
  b. Setup
  c. Adjustments
  d. Minor stoppages
  e. Reduced speed
  f. Scrap

Level 4

- Team members understand equipment improvement control and equipment maintenance control.
- Equipment efficiency is 85 percent.

Level 5

- The team is using equipment improvement control and equipment maintenance control.
- Total equipment efficiency is greater than 95 percent.

Our maintenance organization had always been problematic. I think it comes from the name "maintenance"—to maintain. It doesn't sound like something that is very progressive. However, our total productive maintenance (TPM) program has changed that. It has given a direction beyond doing preventive maintenance. The direction now is what can be done to always have the equipment ready to run and in peak condition. A recent development has been the start of using overall equipment effectiveness (OEE) as a measure of performance. I might add that this measure was impossible for us a year ago due to lack of information needed to calculate an OEE. The most exciting thing to date for me is that our machine operators are the key to this program. They have learned to assess the performance of the machines and direct their maintenance.

Key 8 - Perform Value Analysis of Operations

Any motion, step, or material in the manufacturing process that does not add value to the product is wasteful. Value analysis is a method of reducing waste by analyzing the value of each step, motion, or material.

Level 1

- No understanding of waste.
- No interest in value analysis; a "shotgun" approach to improvements.

Level 2

- The identification of non-value-adding steps has started.
- All employees share a common understanding of waste and the use of a Treasure Map.

Level 3

- Elimination or modification of non-value-adding steps has started the use of a Treasure Map.
- The actual work ratio is 70 percent non-value-added and 30 percent value-added.

Level 4

- The actual work ratio is 50 percent non-value-added and 50 percent value-added.

Level 5

- Although lot sizes and product types change constantly, the actual work ratio is 30 percent non-value-added and 70 percent value-added.

Here is where our cost accounting group has been an incredible support. Our old cost accounting methods allocated overhead based on direct labor. Our direct labor is only 8 percent of sales, so that was a lot of cost allocated across products. To deal with this, we have adopted an activity-based costing system. More recently, individual operations are now developing their own activity models. These models have provided a blueprint for eliminating non-value-added activities (NVA).

Key 9 - Concurrent Engineering

As you can see, there are no definitions for the 5 levels of this key. For our situation it was not enough to talk about the customer's role in product design. We need to focus in on tools to reduce design lead time, getting to what the customer wants quicker, and transferring that technology from a development phase to a manufacturing phase quicker. That's the fun of continuous improvement—when your strategies are not working, you have got to move on.

Key 10 - Develop Quick Changeover Technology

Today's customers demand that a supplier be flexible enough to produce a great variety of parts in small volumes. Reducing changeover time allows a manufacturer to cost-effectively produce in small volumes.

Level 1

- Current operating belief holds that lot sizes should be large enough to reduce the number of changeovers.

Level 2

- Some employees have received quick changeover training.
- Setup time on all bottleneck equipment has been reduced by 90 percent.

Level 3

- All manufacturing employees have received quick changeover training.
- Setup time on all processing equipment has been reduced by 90 percent.

Level 4

- Setup time is reduced to under 10 minutes on all processing equipment.

Level 5

- Changeover time is less than or equal to the time required to produce one cycle or part.

The key to this has been Shigeo Shingo's SMED system. That gave us the methodology we needed to implement. I mentioned our overall pilot results on all equipment and how we reduced setup time to under 2 hours. Getting setup times under 10 minutes has been pretty much a part-by-part process, but we have been able to transfer technology to get across-the-board results.

Key 11 - Improve Production Scheduling

Effectively communicating realistic schedules that smooth the periods of confusion or unnecessary idleness is the necessary ideal manufacturing environment.

Level 1

- Completions are less than 50 percent on time.

Level 2

- Completions are more than 50 percent on time.
- The company uses daily part number schedules to satisfy monthly completion plans.

Level 3

- Completion delays are predictable; arrangements are made with customers to minimize ill effects.
- Completions to part number schedules are at least 75 percent on time.
- Performance to production plan is 100 percent ± 5 percent.

Level 4

- Completions to part number schedules are at least 90 percent on time.
- Performance to production plan is 100 percent ± 2 percent.

Level 5

- All completions are on time with no last-minute chaos.

This was a significant challenge to us. We had a centralized scheduling system that was flawed; manufacturing always had a complaint that the scheduling was unrealistic. So, we began to educate all of our team leaders on material planning and scheduling to begin developing their own operation plans. We have a long way to go but now we have 100 percent compliance to production plan rates, and 94 percent of our part numbers are on time, while premium freight has been reduced by 90 percent.

Key 12 - Reduce Total Inventory: Raw Materials, WIP, Finished Goods

Large inventories are "Band-Aids" that hide problems in the manufacturing process. Cutting inventory uncovers those problems, revealing a team's opportunities for improvement. Reducing inventory is also the most effective way to shorten lead times and improve quality. In any process where product moves from one operation to the next, cutting inventory proportionally shortens the time required to move product through those operations (for example, a 50 percent inventory reduction shortens lead times by 50 percent).

Level 1

- Inventory is considered a necessary evil; thus, there is no interest in reducing it.

Level 2

- A partial approach to reducing inventory throughout the entire factory has begun.

Level 3

- The team's total inventory (WIP and finished goods) does not exceed 5 days.
- The ration of WIP to finished goods is 40:60.

Level 4

- Small-lot production begins (SMED).
- The WIP to finished goods ratio is 30:70.
- WIP and finished goods do not exceed 3 days.

Level 5

- Proper inventory control methods and machinery are in place.
- Improvement and evaluation systems are perfected.
- The team makes exactly the right product at exactly the right time to fill the customer's need.

This key is what shows us how well our planning systems are working, and how well we are able to execute those plans. Presently our inventory turns are over 30, compared to an industry standard of 9, but we know there is a lot of opportunity to double our turns.

Key 13 - Implement Zero-Monitoring Manufacturing

In a zero-monitoring environment, each team member can run multiple pieces of equipment without having to monitor the machines in process.

Level 1

- No one understands that monitoring and attending are forms of waste.

Level 2

- People are made thoroughly aware of the waste of monitoring and attending equipment.

Level 3

- Some equipment can run unmonitored and unattended through lunch break.

Level 4

- Most machines can run unmonitored and unattended through lunch break.
- Operators are running more machines.
- Many machines are left running when operators leave for home.

Level 5

- Desired output flows are achieved with virtually no monitoring required.

Improvement here has been a big reason why our direct labor has been reduced to less than 8 percent of sales. By having machines that can run automatically, people can manage more than one machine. Some machines have been designed to be set up and even run over the weekend by themselves. I think you can get in trouble with this key. Automation to eliminate people should not be the goal. Rather, automate to avoid having people perform non-value-added activities and let them get on with higher level activities.

Key 14 - Developing Suppliers

A manufacturing company must develop a cooperative relationship with its suppliers so they can strengthen each other.

Level 1

- Supplier relationships are limited to purchasing, inspecting the parts as they come in, and arguing about their value.

Level 2

- The client company provides technical support on request.

Level 3

- Each of the supplier's lines has industrial engineering support from the client company to reduce the number of processing steps and lower other costs through industrial engineering methods.

Level 4

- Supplier development begins with the implementation of a continuous improvement plan.

Level 5

- The supplier achieves Level 4 on all keys.

I don't think that this key should be limited to suppliers. We must always be working with our customers in the same way, which is to listen and understand their needs. We launched a program that is headed by our purchasing group and supported by manufacturing and engineering. The goal is to work with one of our worst suppliers and help them deliver on time and reduce costs. Here's the fun part. We had to approach it from the view of what could *we* change, not how the supplier needed to change. In less than a year, the supplier went from zero on-time deliveries and an average of 5 days late, to 99 percent on time and never more than 1 day late. You don't get those kinds of results by telling a supplier how to run their business. You get results by listening to how you impose inefficiencies. An added bonus was that we avoided a price increase due to the supplier's being able to schedule their shop floor more evenly.

Key 15 - Develop Skill Versatility and Cross-Training

To be able to respond to changes in environment and demand, employees must diversify their job skills. Before team members can even hope to master most of the various manufacturing jobs, the jobs themselves must be simplified. After developing a plan for proper education and training, a cross-training board is posted to track everyone's progress.

Level 1

- Employees have no interest in skill versatility.

Level 2

- Skills needed in each operation have been defined.

Level 3

- Skill training begins with operations.

Level 4

- Teams begin cross-training between operations in their process.

Level 5

- The plant can freely redistribute the work force to adapt to changes.

This has been great in many ways. People have an opportunity to learn new skills, and with that comes a greater self-confidence. We have a 55-year-old grandmother who was terrified to learn computer skills. She begged me not to make her do it. I asked her to give it a couple of weeks. If she didn't like it, she could stop. That same person is now a coordinator for the area she works in to design an activity-based management model. Something we have not dealt with yet is how to redesign our pay system. To reward a multiskilled workforce is great.

Key 16 - Use Mechatronics

Mechatronics, the combining of mechanical and electronic technology, is most commonly used with numerically controlled (NC) equipment. Mechatronics can make complex, time-consuming tasks simpler, faster, and more precise.

Level 1

- Mechatronics are ignored.

Level 2

- Education begins on how mechatronics might be applied.

Level 3

- Mechatronics are used for production activities.
- Management is eager to apply mechatronics.

Level 4

- Mechatronics are used to monitor and control the process.
- Mechatronics are incorporated in factory improvements.
- Inspection is done with poka-yoke devices.

Level 5

- Mechatronics are used wherever they apply.

This has completely changed the way we build tooling. CNC lathes, electronic discharge machines and grinders have gone a long way to reduce the cost of tooling while increasing tool quality and delivery. We have reduced the dollars spent buying tooling on the outside by 75 percent while increasing demand for tooling by 69 percent. Mechatronics also has been vital in the area of process monitoring.

Key 17 - Conserve Energy and Materials

Conserving energy and materials preserves our environment and reduces expenses. Before installing energy-efficient equipment or modifying existing equipment, many companies find great savings through employee participation in energy and materials conservation.

Level 1

- No interest in conserving energy and materials.

Level 2

- Companywide promotion generates interest in conservation.

Level 3

- The company has a general conservation strategy and has begun to follow it.

Level 4

- A majority of conservation goals are achieved while new conservation opportunities are identified.

Level 5

- All conservation goals are achieved.
- The company has developed a second-generation conservation plan.

For us, the energy to produce compressed air is significant. Walking into the plant on Sunday when the machines were down, you would hear air leaking from several sources. This became a target of our TPM program. Another big hitter was the electricity used to heat the furnaces and the use of H_2 gas as a protective atmosphere inside. This has led to significant increases in the efficiency of our furnaces. For example, the need to produce a new furnace was completely avoided as a result of the improvements made to this part of the process.

Key 18 - Develop Site Technology

Site technology is the skills, knowledge, and equipment a team applies to running an operation or process. It is also largely a product of the informal "know-how" of the individuals involved. Because people often move out of jobs where they acquire this know-how, it is important to capture this knowledge to share it with others. In each case, the technology should improve before it is passed on.

Level 1

- No interest in the progress of competitors.

Level 2

- The company sees itself as one step behind the industry, lacking the ability to implement new technology.

Level 3

- The company is on a par with the rest of the industry.

Level 4

- The company is one step ahead of the industry average, able to steadily implement new technology.

Level 5

- The company's site technology is leading the industry.
- Basic and new technologies are leading edge.

This is a topic many of our teams are only now beginning to address. Many have begun to assemble manuals and documents that define how things need to be done, as well as some creative means of making sure they are used. Our approach to technology has always been to be aware of what is going on in our industry and in related industries. We have several people who travel extensively to see what is going on. When they find something to help solve a problem, we begin to get operations people involved. We still have a lot of opportunity to bring in and transfer technology more effectively.

The Keys to Continuous Improvement are like the tools in a toolbox—you don't use all of them all of the time but they all have a purpose and sooner or later you will need them all. Our approach is to read as much as you can, visit as many good companies as you can, and don't talk about it, just do it.

About the Author

Iwao Kobayashi, an industrial consultant well-known in Japan, is the creator of the PPORF 20 Keys program for developing manufacturing companies' core abilities to adapt to change.

Mr. Kobayashi graduated from Shibaura Technical University in 1943 and entered Mitsubishi Heavy Industries. He had been in charge of the design and production department, and established the first mixed-lot automated assembly line in Japan. He also founded new factories and contributed to strengthening the manufacturing constitution of the company by improving shopfloor and production techniques.

During his career at Mitsubishi, Mr. Kobayashi developed a visual control system at the Sagamihara plant, shortened the work-in-process lead time by 75 percent, and increased productivity 100 percent. He visited plants in the United States and Europe, and trained 25 subsidiaries of Mitsubishi Heavy Industries based on his extensive knowledge.

Mr. Kobayashi left Mitsubishi Heavy Industries in 1981 to found the PPORF Development Institute. In his role as head of the Institute he has successfully promoted the improvement of manufacturing quality in more than 150 companies worldwide, including Mitsubishi Agricultural Machinery, Mitsubishi Electric, Akai Electric, Toyo Agricultural Machinery, Sanyo Electric, and Seiko Electronic Industries.

In 1994 Mr. Kobayashi established East Japan PPORF Development Institute as a joint enterprise with Seiko Electronic Industries. He serves as president and a representative director of the new company.

Index

BOOKS FROM PRODUCTIVITY, INC.

Productivity, Inc. publishes books that empower individuals and companies to achieve excellence in quality, productivity, and the creative involvement of all employees. Through steadfast efforts to support the vision and strategy of continuous improvement, Productivity delivers today's leading-edge tools and techniques gathered directly from industry leaders around the world. Call toll-free 1-800-394-6868 for our free catalog.

5 Pillars of the Visual Workplace

The Sourcebook for 5S Implementation

Hiroyuki Hirano

In this important sourcebook recently published by Productivity Press, JIT expert Hiroyuki Hirano provides the most vital information available on the visual workplace. He describes the 5S's: seiri, seiton, seiro, seiketsu, shitsuke (which translate as organization, orderliness, cleanliness, standardized cleanup, and discipline). Hirano discusses how the 5S theory fosters efficiency, maintenance, and continuous improvement in all areas of the company, from the plant floor to the sales office. Presented in a thorough, detailed style, *5 Pillars of the Visual Workplace* explains why the 5S's are important and the who, what, where, and how of 5S implementation. This book includes numerous case studies, hundreds of graphic illustrations, and over forty 5S user forms and training materials.

ISBN 1-56327-047-1 / 353 pages, illustrated / $85.00 / Order FIVE-B258

40 Tools for Cross-Functional Teams

Building Synergy for Breakthrough Creativity

Walter Michalski

Anyone who has tried to build effective cross-functional teams knows that they often fail because they lack the tools, training, and motivation that would enable them to tackle more challenging tasks. From building and sustaining cross-functional teams to recognizing and rewarding them, this book is a complete resource for cross-functional teams.

ISBN 1-56327-198-2 / 160 pages / $30.00 / Order NAV3-B258

The Basics of Cross-Functional Teams

Henry J. Lindborg, Ph.D

If you are a member of a cross-functional team, you will benefit from this quick-read text. This book illustrates what cross-functional teams are, how to be an effective team member, and the many uses of cross-functional teams. These uses include process improvement, benchmarking, FMEAs, and ISO and QS implementation. A process for creating and maintaining cross-functional teams is provided, as well as advice on how to avoid some of the pitfalls and obstacles associated with these teams.

ISBN 0-527-76332-2 / 84 pages / $9.95 / Order QRCFT-B258

The Basics of Idea Generation

Donna Greiner

Generating and implementing ideas are cornerstones for many improvement techniques. This book is a cost-effective way to ensure that your team consistently generates and implements new ideas. Learn how to implement them with a proven five-step process. The author explains 20 tools that help complete each step in the process. You'll also learn solutions to overcoming certain barriers to creativity.

ISBN 0-527-76339-X / 72 pages / $9.95 / Order QRIDEA-B258

Becoming Lean

Inside Stories of U.S. Manufacturers

Jeffrey Liker

Most other books on lean management focus on technical methods and offer a picture of what a lean system should look like. Some provide snapshots of before and after. This is the first book to provide technical descriptions of successful solutions and performance improvements. The first book to include powerful first-hand accounts of the complete process of change, its impact on the entire organization, and the rewards and benefits of becoming lean. At the heart of this book you will find the stories of American manufacturers who have successfully implemented lean methods. Authors offer personalized accounts of their organization's lean transformation, including struggles and successes, frustrations and surprises. Now you have a unique opportunity to go inside their implementation process to see what worked, what didn't, and why. Many of these executives and managers who led the charge to becoming lean in their organizations tell their stories here for the first time!

ISBN 1-56327-173-7 / 350 pages / $35.00 / Order LEAN-B258

Corporate Diagnosis

Setting the Global Standard for Excellence

Thomas L. Jackson with Constance E. Dyer

All too often, strategic planning neglects an essential first step and final step-diagnosis of the organization's current state. What's required is a systematic review of the critical factors in organizational learning and growth, factors that require monitoring, measurement, and management to ensure that your company competes successfully. This executive workbook provides a step-by-step method for diagnosing an organization's strategic health and measuring its overall competitiveness against world class standards. With checklists, charts, and detailed explanations, Corporate Diagnosis is a practical instruction manual. The pillars of Jackson's diagnostic system are strategy, structure, and capability. Detailed diagnostic questions in each area are provided as guidelines for developing your own self-assessment survey.

ISBN 1-56327-086-2 / 115 pages / $65.00 / Order CDIAG-B258

Implementing a Lean Management System

Thomas L. Jackson with Constance E. Dyer

Does your company think and act ahead of technological change, ahead of the customer, and ahead of the competition? Thinking strategically requires a company to face these questions with a clear future image of itself. Implementing a Lean Management System lays out a comprehensive management system for aligning the firm's vision of the future with market realities. Based on Hoshin Management, the Japanese strategic planning method used by top managers for driving TQM throughout an organization, Lean Management is about deploying vision, strategy, and policy to all levels of daily activity. It is an eminently practical methodology emerging out of the implementation of continuous improvement methods and employee involvement. The key tools of this book builds on the knowledge of the worker, multi-skilling, and an understanding of the role and responsibilities of the new lean manufacturer.

ISBN 1-56327-085-4 / 150 pages / $65.00 / Order ILMS-B258

Implementing TPM

The North American Experience

Charles J. Robinson and Andrew P. Ginder

The authors document an approach to TPM planning and deployment that modifies the JIPM 12-step process to accommodate the experiences of North American plants. They include details and advice on specific deployment steps, OEE calculation methodology, and autonomous maintenance deployment. This book shows how to make TPM work in unionized plants and how to position TPM to support and complement other strategic manufacturing improvement initiatives.

ISBN 1-56327-087-0 / 224 pages / $45.00 / Order IMPTPM-B258

JIT Factory Revolution

A Pictorial Guide to Factory Design of the Future

Hiroyuki Hirano

The first encyclopedic picture-book of Just-In-Time, using photos and diagrams to show exactly how JIT looks and functions in production and assembly plants. Unprecedented behind-the-scenes look at multiprocess handling, cell technology, quick changeovers, kanban, andon, and other visual control systems. See why a picture is worth a thousand words.

ISBN 0-915299-44-5 / 218 pages / $50.00 / Order JITFAC-B258

Kaizen for Quick Changeover

Going Beyond SMED

Kenichi Sekine and Keisuke Arai

Especially useful for manufacturing managers and engineers, this book describes exactly how to achieve faster changeover. Picking up where Shingo's SMED book left off, you'll learn how to streamline the process even further to reduce changeover time and optimize staffing at the same time.

ISBN 0-915299-38-0 / 315 pages / $75.00 / Order KAIZEN-B258

Kanban and Just-In-Time at Toyota

Management Begins at the Workplace

Japan Management Association

Translated by David J. Lu

Toyota's world-renowned success proves that with kanban, the Just-In-Time production system (JIT) makes most other manufacturing practices obsolete. This simple but powerful classic is based on seminars given by JIT creator Taiichi Ohno to introduce Toyota's own supplier companies to JIT. It shows how to implement the world's most efficient production system. A clear and complete introduction.

ISBN 0-915299-48-8 / 211 pages / $40.00 / Order KAN-B258

Manufacturing Strategy

John Miltenburg

This book offers a step-by-step method for creating a strategic manufacturing plan. The key tool is a multidimensional worksheet that links the competitive analysis to manufacturing outputs, the seven basic production systems, the levels of capability and the levers for moving to a higher level. The author presents each element of the worksheet and shows you how to link them to create an integrated strategy and implementation plan. By identifying the appropriate production system for your business, you can determine what output you can expect from manufacturing, how to improve outputs, and how to change to more optimal production systems as your business needs changes. This is a valuable book for general managers, operations managers, engineering managers, marketing managers, comptrollers, consultants, and corporate staff in any manufacturing company.

ISBN 1-56327-071-4 / 391 pages / $45.00 / Order MANST-B258

Modern Approaches to Manufacturing Improvement

The Shingo System

Alan Robinson (ed.)

Here's the quickest and most inexpensive way to learn about the pioneering work of Shigeo Shingo, co-creator (with Taiichi Ohno) of Just-In-Time. It's an introductory book containing excerpts of five of his classic books as well as an excellent introduction by Professor Robinson. Learn about quick changeover, mistake-proofing (poka-yoke), non-stock production, and how to apply Shingo's "scientific thinking mechanism."

ISBN 0-915299-64-X / 420 pages / $23.00 paper / Order READER-B258

A Revolution in Manufacturing

The SMED System

Shigeo Shingo

The heart of JIT is quick changeover methods. Dr. Shingo, inventor of the Single-Minute Exchange of Die (SMED) system for Toyota, shows you how to reduce your changeovers by an average of 98 percent! By applying Shingo's techniques, you'll see rapid improvements (lead time reduced from weeks to days, lower inventory and warehousing costs) that will improve quality, productivity, and profits.

ISBN 0-915299-03-8 / 383 pages / $75.00 / Order SMED-B258

TPM in Process Industries

Tokutaro Suzuki (ed.)

Process industries have a particularly urgent need for collaborative equipment management systems like TPM that can absolutely guarantee safe, stable operation. In TPM in Process Industries, top consultants from JIPM (Japan Institute of Plant Maintenance) document approaches to implementing TPM in process industries. They focus on the process environment and equipment issues such as process loss structure and calculation, autonomous maintenance, equipment and process improvement, and quality maintenance. Must reading for any manager in the process industry.

ISBN 1-56327-036-6 / 400 pages / $85.00 / Order TPMPI-B258

TO ORDER: Write, phone, or fax Productivity, Inc., Dept. BK, P.O. Box 13390, Portland, OR 97213-0390, phone 1-800-394-6868, fax 1-800-394-6286. Outside the U.S. phone (503) 235-0600; fax (503) 235-0909. Send check or charge to your credit card (American Express, Visa, MasterCard accepted).

U.S. ORDERS: Add $5 shipping for first book, $2 each additional for UPS surface delivery. Add $5 for each AV program containing 1 or 2 tapes; add $12 for each AV program containing 3 or more tapes. We offer attractive quantity discounts for bulk purchases of individual titles; call for more information.

ORDER BY E-MAIL: Order 24 hours a day from anywhere in the world. Use either address:
To order: service@productivityinc.com
To view the online catalog and/or order: http://www.productivityinc.com

QUANTITY DISCOUNTS: For information on quantity discounts, please contact our sales department.

INTERNATIONAL ORDERS: Write, phone, or fax for quote and indicate shipping method desired. For international callers, telephone number is 503-235-0600 and fax number is 503-235-0909. Prepayment in U.S. dollars must accompany your order (checks must be drawn on U.S. banks). When quote is returned with payment, your order will be shipped promptly by the method requested.

NOTE: Prices are in U.S. dollars and are subject to change without notice.

About the Shopfloor Series

Put powerful and proven improvement tools in the hands of your entire workforce!

Progressive shopfloor improvement techniques are imperative for manufacturers who want to stay competitive and to achieve world class excellence. And it's the comprehensive education of all shopfloor workers that ensures full participation and success when implementing new programs. The Shopfloor Series books make practical information accessible to everyone by presenting major concepts and tools in simple, clear language and at a reading level that has been adjusted for operators by skilled instructional designers. One main idea is presented every two to four pages so that the book can be picked up and put down easily. Each chapter begins with an overview and ends with a summary section. Helpful illustrations are used throughout.

Books currently in the Shopfloor Series include:

5S for Operators

5 Pillars of the Visual Workplace

The Productivity Development Team

ISBN 1-56327-123-0 / 133 pages
Order 5SOP-B258 / $25.00

Quick Changeover for Operators

The SMED System

The Productivity Development Team

ISBN 1-56327-125-7 / 93 pages
Order QCOOP-B258 / $25.00

Mistake-Proofing for Operators

The Productivity Development Team

ISBN 1-56327-127-3 / 93 pages
Order ZQCOP-B258 / $25.00

Cellular Manufacturing

The Productivity Development Team

ISBN 1-56327-213-X / 96 pages
Order CELLP-B258 / $25.00

OEE for Operators

Overall Equipment Effectiveness

The Productivity Development Team

ISBN 1-56327-221-0 / 96 pages
Order OEEOP-B258 / $25.00

TPM for Supervisors

The Productivity Development Team

ISBN 1-56327-161-3 / 96 pages
Order TPMSUP-B258 / $25.00

TPM Team Guide

Kunio Shirose

ISBN 1-56327-079-X / 175 pages
Order TGUIDE-B258 / $25.00

TPM for Every Operator

Japan Institute of Plant Maintenance

ISBN 1-56327-080-3 / 136 pages
Order TPMEO-B258 / $25.00

Autonomous Maintenance

Japan Institute of Plant Maintenance

ISBN 1-56327-082-X / 138 pages
Order AUTMOP-B258 / $25.00

Just-in-Time for Operators

The Productivity Development Team

ISBN 1-56327-133-8 / 96 pages
Order JITOP-B258 / $25.00

Focused Equipment Improvement

Japan Institute of Plant Maintenance

ISBN 1-56327-081-1 / 138 pages
Order FEIOP-B258 / $25.00

Continue Your Learning with In-House Training and Consulting from Productivity, Inc.

Productivity, Inc. offers a diverse menu of consulting services and training products that complement the exciting ideas from our books. Whether you need assistance with long-term planning or focused, results-driven training, Productivity's experienced professional staff can enhance your pursuit of competitive advantage.

Productivity, Inc. integrates a cutting edge management system with today's leading process improvement tools for rapid, measurable, lasting results. In concert with your management team, we will focus on implementing the principles of Value Adding Management, Total Quality Management, Just-In-Time, and Total Productive Maintenance. Each approach is supported by Productivity's wide array of team-based tools: Standardization, One-Piece Flow, Hoshin Planning, Quick Changeover, Mistake-Proofing, Kanban, Problem Solving with CEDAC, Visual Workplace, Visual Office, Autonomous Maintenance, Equipment Effectiveness, Design of Experiments, Quality Function Deployment, and more.

Productivity is known for significant improvement on the shopfloor and the bottom line. Through years of repeat business, an expanding and loyal client base continues to recommend Productivity to their colleagues. Contact us to learn how we can tailor our services to fit your needs.